ALIVE TO

Christopher Herbert has been Anglican Vicar of Bourne in Farnham since 1981, as well as being Director of Post-Ordination Training for Guildford diocese and an honorary Canon of Guildford Cathedral. Before that, he was based in the Hereford diocese, where he worked for a while as a teacher and a youth leader, served as a prebendary of Hereford Cathedral and as Adviser – and then as Director – of Religious Education in the diocese. He is married with two children.

He is author of a number of books, incluing *Be Thou My Vision*, Collins.

ALIVE TO GOD

36 SESSIONS FOR YOUTH & CONFIRMATION GROUPS

Christopher Herbert

COLLINS

Collins Liturgical Publications
8 Grafton Street, London W1X 3LA

Distributed in Ireland by
Educational Company of Ireland
21 Talbot Street, Dublin 1

Available in the United States from
Harper & Row, San Francisco
Icehouse One – 401, 151 Union Street
San Francisco, CA 94111-1299

Collins Liturgical Australia
PO Box 316, Blackburn, Victoria 3130

Collins Liturgical New Zealand
PO Box 1, Auckland

ISBN 0 00 599998 7

First published 1987
© Christopher Herbert 1987

Typographical design by Colin Reed
Typset by Bookmag
Made and printed in Glasgow

Contents

INTRODUCTION

Who me? How can I take a confirmation class? 7	Other learning techniques 16
The size of the group 9	Using the Scriptures 16
The setting 9	Using prayer 19
Timing of classes 10	Using church buildings and people 20
Duration of the course 10	A weekend away 21
Planning the session 11	The Confirmation Service and First Communion 23
What did I learn? 12	And what happens when the course is completed? 23
Using games and role plays 13	

I. THE LIFE OF JESUS

1 Pictures of God 27	7 Stepping in the shoes 43
2 Questions of God 29	8 Jesus the healer 45
3 Arguments for God 31	9 The Transfiguration of Jesus 47
4 Knowledge of God 34	10 Jesus the story-teller 49
5 Putting a face on God: Jesus 37	11 The beginning of the end 51
6 A day in the life 40	12 The last days 53

II. THE LIFE OF THE CHURCH

1 The Holy Spirit 57	8 The Sacraments The Eucharist: Bread 79
2 How the Church began 60	
3 The nature of the Bible 62	9 The Sacraments The Eucharist: Wine 81
4 How the Bible came to us 65	
5 The Old Testament 70	10 The Prayer Books 83
6 The New Testament 73	11 The Church's timetable 85
7 The Sacraments: Baptism 75	12 The Anglican Church now 87

CONTENTS

III. THE LIFE OF A CHRISTIAN

1 Prayer and worship	93
2 Rules for living: the Ten Commandments	95
3 Rules for living: the Beatitudes/Summary of the Law	97
4 Forgiveness	99
5 The new way	101
6 The great divide?	103
7 Telling the truth	105
8 Sharing gifts	107
9 Death and life eternal	108
10 'I believe'	110
11 I belong	112
12 Into the future . . .	114

Appendix   117
Acknowledgements   127

Introduction

Who me? How can I take a confirmation class?
If you find yourself facing the task of confirmation training and you are on the look-out for a new way of approach which will be both enjoyable and challenging, look no further. Here is a book which is packed with information about methods of teaching young people, and which also has thirty-six sessions brimming over with ideas for you to adapt and use.

But perhaps that's not your need. Maybe you are looking for something to use with young people in a discussion group or youth club. Here too you may well find ideas which will bring added interest to your work.

This book is based on a year's course covering three main areas: The Life of Christ, The Life of the Church, The Life of the Christian. You can take them in any order you like, and although the course lends itself to continuous use it would be perfectly possible to lift ideas from it to suit your own local needs. It really is meant to be as flexible as that.

Working with young people seems to worry many adults. They shy away from it, assuming that they will not be able to keep order, or not know what to say, or be on the wrong wavelength. It's a shame. There can be no more enjoyable occupation than working with young people when all goes well – when questions are shared, when there's laughter, amusement and good discussion. How can you change from thinking that working with young people is a matter for apprehension to the point where you positively look forward to it? The change required is not as enormous as you might think. It depends largely, though not entirely, on three things. Firstly on whether you believe that what you are trying to convey is important; secondly on whether you are happy with the material you use; and thirdly on your willingness to learn from your own experience both of the past and the present. Let's take those three things a stage further.

It's quite clear that the best teachers are those who are genuinely enthusiastic about their subject. Think back to your own teachers and you will remember with gratitude those who shared their excitement with you. If you are pleased and interested to share your understanding of the Christian faith with young people, they will willingly respond. 'Caught and not taught' may be over-simple but it is close to the truth. However, one of the causes of enthusiasm is the knowledge that you have the subject 'mastered' and when it comes to Christianity that raises a

INTRODUCTION

major problem. No one can possibly claim to have mastered all that there is to know about Christianity, but what you can do, what anyone can do, is to be reasonably confident about certain areas of the faith. Then, if you are faced with questions outside your field, acknowledge your limitations, that's far simpler and far more honest than trying to bluff your way through.

In this book the material is arranged carefully and in such a way that it should be well within anyone's grasp. As long as you prepare each session carefully you should be fine, and that preparation will increase your confidence and skill.

But perhaps the greatest skill required by any youth leader is the ability to evaluate how you as a leader are performing and to learn not only from those sessions which are successful but from those which are disastrous. 'Time spent on reconnaissance is never wasted' is an old and wise motto; there should be a similar one which says 'Time spent on evaluation is the quickest method of improvement'.

If you have enthusiasm for the subject, if you have prepared carefully and if you are willing to evaluate as you go along, your enjoyment, and the enjoyment of your group, is bound to grow.

But what of the young people you are wanting to teach? What do they think? Well, let's be clear. In the age-range thirteen to fifteen they are in the throes of adolescence. At times they will surprise you (and themselves) by their maturity, at others by their childishness. They need to be given confidence to express themselves (they hate to make fools of themselves in front of their friends), they need to be given room to experiment with new ideas and yet also be given the assurance that when they need to they can touch base. Think of them as having grown up in a castle surrounded by concentric walls: there will be times when they need to stay right in the centre and not move at all; there will be occasions when you need to encourage them to explore, and yet other situations in which you will find that they've galloped away into the far distance. It's no wonder that fantasy games of the Dungeons and Dragons variety are so popular at this age. Be prepared then for times of exploration but also for the need to retreat. Treat them at all times with respect and humour and, as far as their Christian faith is concerned, don't be over-zealous about packing too much in their kit-bags. Their pilgrimage, their Christian adventures, will continue long after they have left you; what you are helping to provide is an outline map for some of the journey, emergency rations and sustenance, and a set of skills to help them cope with whatever they may encounter.

Now let's get down to some basic and practical details of how this confirmation course can work . . . First of all:

INTRODUCTION

The size of the group
There are certain 'laws' about group behaviour which are useful to know. A group of between seven and nine is the most effective size, go beyond that and not everyone will feel a sense of membership. Whether you have a mixed group of boys and girls will depend on local circumstances. 'Co-education' is an orthodoxy not to be lightly cast aside but you may well find that single-sex groups at this age also have much to be said for them. When you have decided on the size and composition of the group the next thing to consider is the place where you will meet . . .

The setting
The actual meeting place which you choose for the group is very important. It needs to be reasonably comfortable, well-lit, arranged in such a way that you can see all of the young people and they can see you, and with enough space for everyone. The vestry is unlikely to be the best place for this, somehow vestries are never very welcoming and never seem to have adequate furniture. Certainly try to avoid having a small group in a large hall. It's hopeless. The young people feel vulnerable; you feel conspicuous and the whole thing becomes dismal. Try using the lounge or the dining room of your own house. A domestic atmosphere means that the sessions are not branded as "lessons" and the group doesn't feel like a "class", and you feel more "at home".

The *seating arrangements* too are important. If you want them to write will they need tables or boards on which to rest their note books? Can they write comfortably without being overlooked? Sort out these kinds of details first. They may seem trivial at this stage, but the actual management of a group depends much more upon these things than you might imagine.

So: let's assume that you have thought about the room. Everything is arranged as you want it and you are now waiting for your first customers to arrive. Again, it's very obvious, but do make sure that you *greet them*, make them feel welcome and if they don't know each other introduce them – but not formally. The chances are that when they have taken their seats – whether it be on chairs or on the floor – they will see that as their space from now on. Nothing unusual in that, we all do it, but be aware of it and make sure that the territories aren't so rigidly defined that anyone feels excluded.

There they are then, in your house, sitting around waiting for you to begin. It's your big moment. How you begin will set the style and tone of the group for quite a while. If you as the leader are hesitant and self-conscious they will be too, and that's awful. You can feel the temperature rising. They need you to be in charge, calmly and confidently: they need you to put them at their ease. That confidence,

INTRODUCTION

of course, takes a long while to develop. Don't expect it to be established from the very first second. It will grow gradually as the group progresses, provided that they feel able to trust and depend on you. One of the components of that trust is your ability to manage time, and it's to that that we now turn.

Timing of classes

You will know how uneasy and annoyed you feel if you have been at a meeting which goes on and on and on. Everyone wants the Chairman to call a halt but he seems oblivious to time passing. Young people have the same feelings. They too need to know the time the session begins and the time it ends. It gives proper boundaries to the event so that if they are bored they know how long they've got to survive. One of the regular and justifiable complaints of young people is about adults who go on longer than they should. Perhaps it's their scoutleader who says, "Before we finish we'll just do that one more time" and repeats the phrase again ten minutes later; or perhaps it's a teacher at school: "He never lets us out until long after the bell goes." Of course in either case the adult in charge may have good reason, but the general point remains valid. Good time-keeping makes for a good session; there's a kind of 'contract' involved and to break it is very unhelpful.

So, how do you actually manage to keep an eye on the time and manage it to everyone's satisfaction? If there's a clock in the room position it where you can see it; or wear a wrist-watch and refer to that. But don't appoint one of the group to be a time-keeper – that distracts him or her from the task in hand. It's your job to manage the time on behalf of the group and to ensure that the session comes to a proper conclusion at the right moment. If you can do that, and it's a skill that comes with practice, you will be well on the way to running a happy group.

How *long* each lesson should last is something to which you need to give attention. Most schools operate on a forty minute basis. This isn't simply because it's administratively convenient but because it also matches the attention span of most adolescents. You do not want your confirmation or discussion group to be too much like school but you will probably find that forty-five minutes is about the right length of time required. Once you have decided on the time-boundaries make sure that everyone else knows what they are, not least the parents if they have to turn out to collect their youngsters at the end of each session.

Duration of the course

If timing each individual session is important so is the length of the course. This is bound to vary from parish to parish and depends to a great extent upon whether the children and young people have taken part in pre-confirmation activities. In an ideal world Church education should begin with the provision of a creche for babies, have Sunday Schools for the young children, clubs for older ones and discussion groups for adults. Within that kind of framework confirmation would fit easily. It is part of a long process. However, ideal worlds are just that – ideal. You are the only one who can judge how long your confirmation training should last. Some parishes use a three-year scheme with confirmation coming somewhere in the middle; others have a one-year scheme with carefully organised pre-confirmation groups and post-confirmation clubs and activities. It's very unlikely that a six or ten session confirmation course can offer much of value; there's hardly time for the young people to know each other or for you to know them. A school year, that is, three terms of about 'twelve' weekly sessions each, is probably a reasonable span at which to aim.

So, before you begin, you will need to discuss your particular parish circumstances with the Vicar, the Sunday School teachers and the youth leaders. Find out what syllabus and books the Sunday School have been using. You don't want to go in for too much repetition (Oh the poor Good Samaritan: the story seems to be done by all ages all the time); on the other hand re-inforcement is an accepted method of learning. Have a talk to the youth leaders to see how confirmation might fit in with their programmes. You will need to discover whether they see their clubs as essentially 'social' or, if there is a teaching element, how confirmation may relate to it. Ask the Vicar some questions too. Find out how he sees the educational pattern of the parish and, perhaps more importantly, his attitude to young people taking an active and lively part in the worship of the church. If the church is 'dead' for young people, no matter how well you conduct confirmation training the leaving rate will be high. When you have done all that, you will be in a better position to judge how long the confirmation course itself should last and of what it should consist.

> **A SUMMARY**
> So far we have dealt with the practical details of confirmation training: the size of the group; the place of meeting; the duration of the classes; and the length of the course. Let's move now to some components of the 'sessions'.

Planning the session
Planning the session in some detail is vital, but how do you go about it? Each session should have an *aim* to give it direction and purpose. It's an old and tried method, but good nonetheless. (You'll notice that all the examples of sessions which follow in this book have an aim.) Whatever your aim is, try to write it out in ten words and no more than ten words. That's a golden rule. You'll ignore it at your peril.

INTRODUCTION

Having written down the aim, then ask yourself another question: "How can that aim best be fulfilled?" You are now beginning to think of the content of the session: so pay attention to the *materials* you will want to use. Suppose, for example (and the example is an easy one), that for part of the session you want the young people to write: do you have enough pencils and paper for everyone? All right, it's very obvious but if you are not well-prepared in this way the session can easily go adrift.

Now ask yourself another question: "What do I hope the young people will *learn* in this session?" The temptation in answering this is to be vague and say something like: "I hope they will learn to be kind." Maybe that's a worthy hope but it's doomed as a session basis. Be more specific and don't have too many expectations. If they learn three things in one session you will have achieved a great deal.

What did I learn?

And finally, when the session is over, the young people have gone home and you are sitting in your favourite arm-chair taking a deep breath, conduct a session post-mortem. Were the aims achieved? Was the aim fulfilled in the way you expected? Were the materials adequate? What did the young people learn? What did you learn – about them? about the topic? about how to get across to them? And before you reach for an invigorating cup of coffee, make careful notes about the session ready for next time, analysing what went well and what went badly. It's a little time-consuming but the effort involved is well worthwhile, for in this way you are gradually developing your own expertise.

Let's *re-cap* for the moment about planning a session:

Firstly: state your aim in not more than ten words
Secondly: ask yourself the question "How can that aim best be fulfilled?"
Thirdly: give careful thought to the materials you will need
Fourthly: ask "What do I hope the young people will learn?"
Fifthly: ask "What did I learn?"

Let's sound a warning shot at this stage. Planning sessions is important, of that there can be no question: however, if a session is to be really successful it requires give and take on both sides. In other words, *be flexible*. Be prepared to abandon your plan if you feel that the youngsters have brought up a subject which needs further exploration: be prepared to let the session develop a life of its own: don't stick absolutely rigidly to your aim. If you do, you guarantee failure. Somehow what you want to achieve is a balance between a planned session and spontaneous input from the youngsters. The balance is not easily achieved as any experienced teacher will tell you. Sometimes sessions which are planned to the last detail go brilliantly and at other times they die the death. Sometimes the completely unplanned session is sparkling and at other times it reverts to aimless meanderings. It's unlikely that any leader has ever taken part in the perfect session: perhaps "good enough" is the highest any of us ever achieve. If there's such a thing as "planned spontaneity" then maybe that's what we're after.

Using games and role plays
Have you noticed what people do when they discuss their holidays? They skip the happy parts, the safe journey, the clean beaches, the good food, but give you in great detail something which went disastrously wrong. Maybe it was the breakdown on the motorway ("We waited ages and ages. All that traffic whizzing by, and the baby crying to be fed in the back seat. And then a police car drew up. Were we relieved to see them? A young officer came over to us, I can see him now – dark brown eyes and a gorgeous smile; one of his teeth was crooked though . . ."); or perhaps it was a dramatic sea-rescue or even, in the tradition of French farce, a mix-up over the bedrooms. Whatever it was, the sheer drama of the situation will have made the details stick in their memory.

The fact that we human beings remember and learn from the dramatic and ignore the humdrum has led to a good deal of experimentation in teaching. Amongst those experiments are role plays and educational 'games', used now in a wide variety of places. The purpose of these 'games' and 'plays' is to help the participants learn from their own experience. It isn't just a question of making remembering easier; it's more important than that. Role plays and games are ways of taking experience seriously, ways of enabling young people to develop confidence in their own learning.

You may not have played such games before and you may feel that a more traditional approach (it's called 'Chalk and Talk' in the trade) would be easier. Don't give up before you start. Games are just that – games. They are enjoyable and fun. But if you are to ensure that they work you will need to experience them yourself. How can you do this? You could invite a few of your friends to take part. You could approach your Diocesan Youth Officer or the Local Education Authority youth office to ask them for help. It's quite likely that they will know of groups who use games for learning and they could introduce you to them. In other words, if you are going to use games then you should take the plunge. Don't try to short-circuit this advice by using the games with the young people without having tried them yourself. That's not fair, and what's more leaves you unable to understand what it feels like to be them. No, take playing games as an educational

INTRODUCTION

tool seriously; it will open your eyes and bring a zest to your teaching and learning you didn't think possible.

In the sessions which follow a considerable range of games is suggested. They are not meant to be exhausting or exhaustive. In preparing the session, consider what games you would like to use. Invent some yourself if you like, but do remember that as the leader of the group you should not take part in the game. Your job is to enable the group to function and you should stand on the edge of the activity giving confidence and support. And when the game has ended, it is your job to discover what the participants feel that they have learnt from it. You may ask questions but should not supply the answers. You must also supply the boundaries of the game, either the physical boundaries ("Nobody is to go beyond the door"), or the time boundaries ("The game will finish at . . ."). It's when the game has finished that you really come into your own. Then you will have to keep a fairly firm control because most participants like to slip back into the game they've been playing, or if a role play, back into the character. You are there to help them to distance themselves very slightly from the role, from the game, so that they can see what was actually going on.

How does all this work in practice? Firstly, *a role play*. Let's describe what it is. A role play is an unscripted, unrehearsed piece of drama in which the participant, as it were, steps into the shoes of a character and allows that character to develop and change as he goes along. The purpose of the role play is to increase understanding; to see what it feels like to be someone else.

If you look at the session headed "Stepping in the shoes . . .", (page 43), you will see that it is based on a well-known Bible story: the healing of the paralysed man. Although the attention focusses on that man and on Jesus there are a number of other people involved about whom the Bible story says nothing. Isn't that a pity? This is where role play can be so enjoyable and so enlightening. Imagine that you are the owner of the house. You haven't long lived there, you've had to work very hard to raise enough money to purchase the house. To your delight you discover that Jesus is coming to visit . . .

You should now have enough information to help you into the part. You can imagine the pride of ownership. You can imagine your feelings as the crowds begin to develop. ("Mind the paintwork!") and the exhilaration as Jesus comes through the door. So, there you are sitting at his feet; outside there's some scuffling, occasional shouts . . . and then thumps and bangs on the roof overhead . . .

If this were a role play the participant would be encouraged to talk aloud, to tell his story, and your job as the leader might be to ask a few radio-interview kind of

INTRODUCTION

questions. "How long had you lived there? What were your feelings when . . .?" You know the sort of thing. Or, instead of an interview, you could set up the role play so that the householder, having encouraged his wife to go shopping for the day, tries to explain to her when she comes home what has happened . . .

Whatever method you choose, remember that you are there to enable the role play to happen. You must give confidence and freedom to the participants and allow the play to go where it will. You cannot guarantee the outcome of the role play, that is in the hands of the characters; but you can help the participants to see what it was like to be in that sort of situation.

So, remembering that you are there to provide the time-boundaries, call a halt when you feel the time is right. Then, as it is your task as leader to help the participants to learn from the role play, explain carefully that the role play is over and that now the time has come to assess and learn from what has taken place. Begin with the role players. They have risked themselves publicly on behalf of the group, thank them for that and ask them how they felt it had gone. What had they actually learnt? Did they feel understood, threatened, worried, happy? In other words help them gradually to leave the role. Then bring in the rest of the group: What did they observe? What did they learn? What insights do they now have about the biblical episode? When the questions are exhausted you can then either leave the role play or go back into it and develop it further. If you do this don't forget that 'de-briefing' at the end is very important. Always allow time for that to take place.

So much for role plays. What about *educational games?* If you look at the lesson headed 'The Holy Spirit', (page 57), you will see the bare bones of an educational game. Again the intention is for the participants to learn from their own experience, to assess and analyse what takes place and, in confirmation classes, to relate that learning to their Christian growth. As in the role plays you will need to set the boundaries of time and place. You will need to set the game in motion, to give confidence to the players, to enable them to learn. Explain at the beginning what the educational game is: for example: "Imagine that this room is an island. No one can leave and no one can arrive. You have landed on this island after a shipwreck and you expect to be stranded for some weeks. You have to work out between you how you will survive . . . because we haven't got time to spare I'm going to speed up the time and tell you at regular intervals what day it is and what time it is . . . but apart from that I hope not to interfere with the game as it progresses . . .". And then you allow the game to develop.

You'll see from the description that the game is a 'lift' from *Lord of the Flies*, but you can decide to approach the analysis of the game when it is over from any

15

INTRODUCTION

number of angles. For example you could ask them to assess how 'rules' were made and how they were enforced; you could look at the way leadership developed and how authority was established . . . the possibilities are virtually endless. But let's get back to the session . . .

Imagine that the game has gone on for twenty or thirty minutes (or less or more) and you decide to call a halt. Do just that. Call the room to order, explain that the game has now ended and that everyone must try to step away from the game and look at it as though they were watching a film. Begin by asking the major participants how they thought the game had developed. Who did what, when? Move on from that chronological assessment to the feelings of the participants: who was delighted/worried/angry/happy? Allow those feelings to be expressed in such a way that the game does not re-start (not as easy as it sounds: feelings are very powerful and go on slopping around like water in a tank long after the tank itself has come to rest); and then move from the feelings into raising awareness about the underlying issues. If 'authority' seems to have been the major issue ask how their understanding of 'authority' compares with, say, that of Jesus, or if 'rules' have been the issue, how the rules on the island compare with the rules of the Old and New Testaments. When all that is over and the discussion finished, don't forget to *thank* everyone for taking part. Young people are very trusting and your thanks for being entrusted with that task must be expressed, loudly and clearly.

There you are, then, two important and helpful educational tools: role plays and games. They are not easy to use but your skill as leader will develop with practice. Don't expect the plays and games to be a success from the word 'go', but build on your experience, try new methods and new ways of learning, and you will discover that your teaching (and your own self-understanding) will improve steadily and surely.

Other learning techniques
There are, in the sessions which follow, a number of role plays and games but there are also other techniques as well. The creation of collages (lots of photographs on a theme cut from magazines); poetry; stories; music-making and music listening. All of these are perhaps more commonly used than games and role plays, this doesn't mean however that they need any less preparation. Do check before each session begins that the practical techniques suggested are ones with which you are familiar.

Using the Scriptures
Unless your young people are very unusual it is safe to assume that their knowledge of the Bible will be quite limited. They will know that it is a book, but

may not be aware that it is more like a library than a single volume. They will know that there is an Old Testament and a New Testament but probably not be aware of the difference between them. They will know the more popular stories: Noah, David and Goliath, Moses and the Bullrushes and, of course, the Good Samaritan. In other words, the Bible is not a book to which they have been introduced systematically or carefully. Don't despair. You may be comforted to know that when Bishop Ridley went to the English diocese of Gloucester in the middle of the sixteenth century he found that of his 311 clergy, 171 were unable to recite the Ten Commandments, 33 did not know where in their Bibles to find them, 30 did not know where in their Bibles to find the Lord's Prayer and 27 did not know who was its author. The young people you teach are likely to be better informed than those clergy.

You will see that in the sessions which follow four are devoted to the Bible itself and they, in a simple way, will provide some of the information young people need. More about that later. But in the other sessions of the course biblical material is also important. How can you use this material?

The first thing to establish is that each young person should *bring a Bible* with them to every session. The version of the Bible chosen is up to you. If you are looking for simplicity of approach either the *Good News Bible* or the *New International Version* could be suggested; if you prefer something a little more 'middle-of-the-road' you could use either the *New English Bible* or the *Jerusalem Bible*; if you are concerned for literary quality and accuracy then the *Revised Standard Version* is probably the best compromise. You may well find that the youngsters use the *Good News Bible* or the *New English Bible* at school. There's no need to be rigid about which version you use, in fact the sheer variety available can be eye-opening, but if you want to study the text verse by verse it is worth having a stock of the same version available to hand out. The Bible Society gives discounts on bulk orders and you may find that your Church Council will be willing to pay for a set of Bibles for your class.

Having chosen which version you will use, how do you go about using the Scriptures in confirmation groups? To begin with you need to establish that the Bible is a source-book, and should be treated as such. Familiarity with its layout is essential, and you can play quiz-games (e.g. Lesson II:3) to enable the young people to feel more at home with it. Then you need to show how the Bible itself came to be constructed; how over the years groups and individuals contributed to it. (*God Speaks to You*: 2 vols., Collins is an excellent handbook for this – and ought to be available as a reference.) Thirdly, you must encourage the young people to treat the Bible intelligently. As a book it has been subjected to the most scrupulous and interesting research for many years and that research has led to all

INTRODUCTION

kinds of new understandings. Whilst the Bible is undoubtedly sacred and undoubtedly a means for God to disclose himself to us, that does not mean that it should be treated unintelligently. Quite the reverse. We have an obligation as Christians to search for truth and no good scholarship should give us cause for alarm. In all those respects then, the Bible is like any other collection of books – open to scrutiny, to debate, to enquiry. But unlike any other collection of books in the Western world the Bible has been regarded as being of the greatest and most important significance. It's the one book which every family is likely to possess; the one book assumed to be on the 'Desert Island'*; the one book upon which the most solemn vows are made.

The Bible is called, with great simplicity and power, "The Word of God". For this reason, as well as being approached intellectually, it needs to be treated as a spiritual treasure-house. This is not to say that God is not met through the intellect, that would be absurd, but the Bible does touch at levels deeper than the intellect. It speaks to the very core of our being. Somehow then, as teachers, we have to find ways of using the Scriptures with young people which encourage them in serious intellectual enquiry but which at the same time allow them to be moved in their hearts. Not easy. What can we do?

It will be the way we treat the Bible which will convey this more than anything else. Treat it casually and the young people will treat it casually too. Treat it over-solemnly and they will be puzzled. You set the style of approach by encouraging honest and sensitive exploration.

Let's take a lesson as an example – and see how this can be done. If you look at Lesson I.8 you will see that it involves the account in Mark's Gospel of the calming of the storm and the healing of the man called 'Legion' (Mark 4:35-5:20). Begin by reading the story aloud. If there is a very good reader in the group ask him or her to read it, but if not, read it out loud yourself. (By the way, do be careful about who you ask to read. There may well be someone in the group who has great difficulty in reading, and so the traditional 'reading around the group' can cause acute discomfort. You are not trying to improve reading skills, you are trying to get them to hear the story afresh).

When you have read the story (and do look up from the book as you are reading, it holds attention) suggest a period of quiet when they either think about the story or read it through again for themselves. You then need to take them through the layers of the story. Begin with Mark as an editor/author: "Why do you think Mark put those two stories close together? Do they shed light on each other?" Then move on to the straightforward historical question: "Do you think this happened

*A popular BBC radio programme.

as described?" And then ask for the reasons for their answers. Move on down the layers by moving attention towards Jesus and the classic question: "What kind of person must Jesus have been to have such stories told about him?", and then deepen further by saying something like: "We have now investigated these stories as carefully as we can, but these stories aren't just history. They speak to us today. I'm now going to read the story again, afterwards there will be silence for a while, and I want you simply to allow something in the story to catch your attention. It might be the storm. It might be the disciples. It might be something Jesus said. Whatever it is, and it will be different for each one of you, day-dream about that, play around with it and ask God to help you understand what you should learn from it . . . ." It's so difficult to put this into words and you will have to find your own way of doing it, but what you are after is a quiet deepening of their understanding, and a way to help them move through the layers of the story.

This isn't the only way of handling the Scriptures, and it would be wrong to use this method every time. There is room for drama; for straightforward discussion; for role play; for music. You will be able to decide which method suits which occasion. What you will discover – all teachers do – is that your own understanding will be increased and deepened as you go along. Teaching can be the most effective way of learning.

Using prayer
There is some evidence that young people pray much more often than we might imagine. Admittedly that prayer is rarely public and rarely discussed. An activity so private, so intense, deserves a proper reticence. But their need to pray also deserves recognition, and within confirmation sessions we should be providing the means to help them continue praying. There's no need to tackle this head on, much will be learnt from how you as leader conduct prayers, the relationship with God you seem to have and, that word much beloved of young people, your 'sincerity'.

It is good to begin each session with prayer, to commend the learning to God, to ask God's guidance and blessing. How you pray is up to you. You could either use a well-known prayer e.g. 'O most merciful redeemer, friend and brother . . .'. or pray extempore. Don't be over-long in the prayer and don't use prayer as a means of preaching. That is a horrible travesty. It's the same at the conclusion of the session, gather up all you have learnt and offer it to God. Again, whether you use your own words or someone else's does not really matter, though a balance between the two is probably best. You may find that you need a book of prayers to help you, for example, Giles Harcourt's *Short Prayers for the Long Day* (Collins) or *Prayers for use at Alternative Services* (Mowbrays). But if you use written prayers do try to make them your own: use them in your own devotions until they are second-nature to you. As well as written prayers or extempore prayers, do, if you can, introduce the young people to silence both at the beginning and at the end of the class. At first the silence is likely to be very brief (tell them the duration of the silence before you begin so that they know what the end-limit is) but after a while you will discover that they can cope with more and more. Explain that in the silence you are waiting on God, being still with him, in the lovely Quaker phrase "centering down". If you think it would help, give them a Biblical text upon which to ponder e.g. "Be still and know that I am God . . .".

You can see that simply in the way you begin and close the sessions you have introduced the young people to three different kinds of prayer: silence, extempore prayer, and the prayers of others. Within the sessions themselves, however, you will need to consider other forms of praying: for example, as Brother Kenneth has suggested, a 'string' prayer. That is, a piece of string, with lots of knots in it to remind you either of people or events for which to pray. It's really a simple version of the rosary. Or there are the more extended kind of meditations made popular during the last twenty years by Michel Quoist; or a more traditional structured approach around the word "ACTS" i.e. Adoration, Confession, Thanksgiving, Supplication. The Church has a remarkably rich heritage of prayers: from the simplicity of "God be in my head" through to the complex and deep approach of *The Cloud of Unknowing*. We owe it to our young people to introduce them to that inheritance . . . .

But ultimately the purpose of prayer is to deepen our awareness of God, to listen, to seek God's will and fulfil it. That's a life-time's occupation but if in confirmation sessions you have sown the seeds of prayer you will have contributed richly to the young people's lives both as they are now and in the future.

Using church buildings and people
One of the richest resources available to us in our work with young people is the church building. In some ways it is so familiar that its potential is over-looked; or if it is used as a resource it is seen simply as a museum: "This is a tomb: that is a pulpit." There's certainly a place for the sharing of information of a factual kind but it should not be done at the expense of a more creative approach. So, what can you do?

You have to think of a way of exploring the church from a different angle, so that the young people can see it with fresh eyes. Perhaps you could get them to visit the building as though they were blind, and to explore it simply with their sense of touch. Or get them to imagine that they are visitors from another planet and they have to send back a report to head-quarters. Or: if there is some animal figure in the painting/statues or stained glass of the church, help them to imagine themselves as that animal and tell the story of the building from that point of view. You could simply allow a feature in the building e.g. a sealed-up door, to be the focus for story-telling. You aren't looking for either moral or religious or improving stories, simply helping the young people to get their imaginations working in the exploration of the building.

This activity could, of course, take up a great deal of time and you may well have friends in the congregation who have special expertise to help you with this part of the programme. Perhaps someone who can explain the history and origins of the parish; someone who knows about the development of stained glass; maybe a heraldry expert or a calligrapher who can help you decipher memorial tablets; or a social historian who can help the young people to see the many roles the church building has played in the community. It may even be possible for the congregation to produce a guide-book for the young people – a way of crossing the generation gap.

The sheer richness and variety of the building and its surroundings, then, can be of enormous interest, but ultimately the building is there to help the community give expression to its beliefs and it's that central fact which the young people will also need to investigate and understand.

So once the building has been thoroughly explored, and all the creative expressions to which it has given rise have been absorbed, the time will come for the people associated with the building to be introduced: the Churchwardens; the organist; the cleaners; the treasurer; the sidesmen and women, in fact anyone who you feel has a sympathetic understanding of youngsters and will be able to show them how their faith and their lives are linked. Only you can know which person in your congregation that is likely to be, and it will be up to you how you set up the meeting; but it will probably work best when the group has been together for a while, is confident, and can welcome another adult into its midst.

A weekend away
One of the insights gained in confirmation training over the past ten years has been about residential week-ends. Some parishes have insisted on at least one such weekend during the training and have found that the weekends have become an invaluable part of the course. The leaders find they have an opportunity to get to know their young people better and the young people find they have a chance to see their leaders in new situations. It really is well worthwhile building in at least one weekend as you plan the confirmation course. If you have little experience of this, ask your diocesan or area youth officer for help.

Then, take your courage in both hands and book the weekend; tell the young people and their parents about your plans well in advance and ask them to keep the dates free. The next stage is to work out what you want to use the weekend for. It could be that you want to spend time using drama or dance or art; or perhaps you want to include an 'adventure' element, climbing or canoeing or caving; or maybe you want to spend more time exploring a biblical theme. But allow time as well for worship, for games, for relaxation, and time for study and discussion. Quite often on conferences it's the casual conversation between meetings which is more important than the meetings themselves.

Work out a timetable for the whole weekend – from the time you arrive until the time you depart. Begin by deciding on mealtimes: when those times are fixed the next priority is to arrange the spaces for recreation; the third stage is to make worship arrangements, and only when all that is done do you arrange the actual content of what you want to study or do. The dangers to be avoided are a too tightly-packed schedule with not enough time to relax and, on the other hand, too loose a programme which loses its aim and purpose. Again you will find that if you need help in structuring such a weekend your youth officer will be pleased to give advice.

The *content* of the weekend will be determined by what you want to achieve, and whether your aims in providing the weekend and the young people's aims in coming, coincide. So, discuss the weekend with them; help them to make suggestions for the weekend, but remember that you too have a responsibility for making the experience enjoyable and worthwhile. Do make sure that the programme is balanced. If you have a predominantly adventure-centred programme, build in time for discussion and reflection. If you have a predominantly study-based programme, make sure that there's plenty of time for games and physical activities.

The *administration* of such a weekend is quite considerable: the numbers coming, the food, the route to be taken, the transport, etc. It can be very helpful therefore to organise the event with a small team of people. One adult to be in charge of all the administration, another to be in charge of food and accommodation and another actually to run the programme. Make certain too that your church backs you in the organisation, and keep them informed of how the plans are going; and when it's all over see that the church is told about the event through a magazine article or something similar.

You will find that you get closer to the youngsters on such a weekend, that you will understand them more fully, and that they, as a group, will come to know and appreciate each other much more as a result. Once the weekend is completed you will discover that it will be the first of many, and a vital part of your confirmation training.

INTRODUCTION

The Confirmation service and First Communion
The relationship between the Confirmation course and the Confirmation service is bound to be a close one. Some opt for the service to be right in the middle of the course, others arrange for the service to be near the end so that there is a sense of a target having been achieved. Whichever of these two options you prefer it is important that the Confirmation service should be seen to be a most significant occasion in the life of the local church. It needs careful preparation for all concerned, including a rehearsal for the candidates. There is much to be said for Deanery Confirmation services either at a local parish church or in the Cathedral, for then the young people gain a sense of belonging not just to the parish but to the wider Christian community as well.

It is also highly important that their First Communion should be a major service. The ideal is either to have a Confirmation service on a Saturday evening followed by First Communion on the Sunday in the candidates' own parish church, with all the parish present to welcome them to the Eucharistic fellowship, or a Confirmation service in the context of the parish Eucharist itself. That can be the time for the giving of a present from the Church to each candidate – a book, for example, or a simple wooden cross.

What you are doing is to affirm the young person as a member of the Church community, a fellow-pilgrim with you in the journey towards God.

And what happens when the course is completed?
So far we have been very practical and concerned ourselves with the various elements of the training course. But what happens when it has been completed? Where this course has been used for Confirmation training you now face a problem. So often once the Confirmation has taken place nothing else happens. It's seen as the end of a process and when it's completed, that's that.

The same is equally true for a non-confirmation course. Where the young people have been meeting regularly for a long period of time and if they've enjoyed each other's company and yours, the chances are that they will want to continue to meet. What can you do then? It is unlikely that you will be able to continue the weekly meetings – but you could try to organise (or better still, persuade someone else to organise) a regular fortnightly or monthly event. A special Youth Communion service on a weekday evening once a month, followed by a discussion or a guest speaker, may well contain the right mix of worship and learning. You could arrange for the discussion to be held in a friend's house, rather than in the church, and also get each member to bring along a named mug for the drinks. It may seem a minor point, but it's that kind of thoughtful detail which helps to make the young people feel part of the Church. How this event is organised will depend upon your circumstances, but a personal letter to each youngster inviting them to the service will be much appreciated and will indicate that they have not been forgotten.

Perhaps a monthly event is impossible. Then you will need to find other means of keeping in touch with the group. Maybe it will be via a youth club, a special interest group, a social evening, a holiday event or a residential weekend. Whatever method best suits your circumstances you will eventually discover. Again this post-confirmation care and training element is one which you will need to discuss in some detail with your Vicar or Parish Council for, in the end, the young people are the responsibility of the whole Church and not simply yours alone.

Ready for the launch
Thirty-six sessions are given, using the style of confirmation preparation recommended in this book. All of them have been used and developed with young people but, as with all lessons, they are not meant to be slavishly copied. They may provide you with a framework and maybe even a few ideas, but you will have to adapt them as you go along to your own circumstances and to the needs of the young people in your group.

I. THE LIFE OF JESUS

I. THE LIFE OF JESUS

1. Pictures of God

Note: Many confirmation courses based on the dictum "Begin where the children are" open the course with a few sessions labelled "Me" or "Myself". There's much to be said for this. However, so many courses at school also begin that way that the youngsters may find it a little jading to start Confirmation sessions in a similar fashion. Try plunging in at the deep end with the following sessions, not about "Me", but about "God".

★ ★ ★ ★ ★

AIM: To understand the symbolism of pictures of God.

EQUIPMENT NEEDED: Bible, felt-tip pens, drawing paper.

Introduction
Having welcomed the young people to their first Confirmation group and got to know their names, explain the rough outline of the course ("Life of Jesus" / "Life of the Church" / "Life of a Christian"), tell them how long the course is going to last, and if they do not already know, how long each session will last. Then ask if they have any questions or any comments they would like to make. In other words, help them to get a sense of the task they are undertaking. If the conversation flows straightaway, fine. Let it do so. If not, don't allow the gaps between the comments to be too long, keep the lesson moving.

Develop from the introductions and giving of 'names', the importance of naming things – and the sheer pleasure of the activity e.g. in giving nicknames. Do they know any traditional nicknames e.g. 'Chalkie' White; or 'Nobby' Clarke? Do their friends have nicknames? Quite often nicknames try to capture a particular characteristic of someone. They are a caricature. So: get them to draw a symbol of a nickname of someone they know. For example, 'Hopalong' might be symbolised by a single boot; or 'Lofty' by a giant. Have a 'guess the nickname' competition.

Then, ask them to move from nicknames and caricatures to something much more difficult. On a blank sheet of paper draw a picture or a symbol of 'God'. (You'll almost hear the youngsters gulp as you ask them to do this, but encourage them . . . .) When the drawings are complete (and explain that you're not looking for a Michelangelo), ask each of them to explain why they have drawn the picture they have. Be sensitive about this and point out that as no one has ever seen God at any time there's no way we can know what God really looks like. Allow the discussion to develop.

Introduce them to the pictures of God in the Old Testament and in particular to Exodus 3:13-14. Get them to think carefully about the "I am" statement and then ask them to try to draw a symbol/picture of God which gets across the profound truth of "I am". It will be difficult, but the exercise will bring much enjoyment and insight.

If you have time you could also look up 1 Kings 19:11-12; Isaiah 6:1-8; Daniel 7:9-10; John 10:7-16; Revelation 1:12-18 to see the different ways all of these authors try to paint a word-picture of God.

Christians believe that Jesus of Nazareth gave us the best 'picture' of God, not only in what he said and did but in who he was. Discuss this if there's time. If not, explain that this will be explored further as the Confirmation sessions go on.

You could round off the session like this. Ask each member of the group to write their name on a sheet of paper, and then, using those names, give thanks to God for them in an extempore prayer.

I. THE LIFE OF JESUS

2. Questions of God

AIM: To explore young people's questions about God. To help them to see that asking questions about God is a good and important activity.

EQUIPMENT NEEDED: Bibles, felt-tip pens, drawing paper, tape-recorder.

Asking questions
Open the conversation with the group by asking if anyone has been somewhere unusual, or has an unusual hobby, or has had an extraordinary experience which they would not mind talking about. Then set up a 'radio' interview with the tape-recorder, inviting one person to be the interviewer and another the interviewee. The interview should not last more than three minutes (you will need a time-keeper). Once the interview is finished ask the group to listen to the recording and to pay particular attention to the questions asked. Discuss with them afterwards which seemed to be the most effective questions. Lead into . . .

Questions of God
Very briefly re-cap the last session: "Pictures of God" and remind the youngsters that any picture of God is bound to be incomplete. No word-picture can tell the whole story, which means that there are always questions to ask. Ask them to imagine that they are working as an interviewer for a local radio station. Their producer wants them to conduct an interview with God, and says that the interview must be serious and touch on the questions everyone would like to pose . . . .

Give everyone a sheet of paper and ask them to write on it the questions they would like to raise either with God or about God. When the lists of questions are finished put them in the centre of the room where everyone can see them and, as a group, put the questions in order of priority. (Note: In similar sessions with young people the questions have varied from: "Who created God?" to "If God isn't married how come Jesus is his Son?")

Then, taking one question at a time, attempt to find a reasonably satisfactory answer to each. For example, if one of the questions is "Who created God?" – and it's almost bound to be – you could suggest that that question has its own answer hidden inside it. If God be God then he is, by definition, the Creator; not a being amongst other beings, but being itself. If God was created then whoever created him must be "God", and so on, back and back, ad infinitum. For God to be God he must be un-created i.e. always have existed, and in that sense, be totally unlike anything or anyone else . . . .

It's obvious when an answer such as that is given, that we are in deep philosophical waters. But that is how it should be. If the conversation about God falters and stutters along, again, that is what should happen. Our language about God is bound to be inadequate, but what you are trying to get across is not only the proper inadequacy of words but also the exhilaration of going on trying to find better means of expression.

If you find this lesson over-difficult you could invite your local Vicar or Minister to attend and ask him or her to try to give some answers to the questions; or get the young people to write a letter containing their questions to the local clergyman asking for a reply for the following week.

You may find that the young people think that their questions are very new. Without in any sense disillusioning them, explain that some of these questions have always puzzled mankind.

Look up Psalm 22 and after giving the background information read it aloud.

Background information: The psalms are a collection of poems and hymns. Some of them are very ancient (although it's difficult to date them accurately). Most scholars agree that the collection was completed by 200 B.C. There is a tradition that King David wrote the psalms, but we have no means of knowing whether or not this is true.

Psalm 22 is probably the prayer of an individual who feels deserted by God (some people have said that the individual represents the nation of Israel, or maybe the king). It has been popular with Christians because it seems to prophesy the sufferings and resurrection of Jesus. Jesus quoted this psalm when he was on the cross: see Mark 15:34.

In reading the Psalm, you will see there is a turning point at verse 21. Up to that verse the man feels abandoned by God in his suffering; but from verse 22 onwards he praises God because he knows that at all times, even in suffering, God will not let him down.

This has been the experience of countless hundreds of Christians. Sometimes they feel that there is no God – but then they become aware that God really is. He does exist. Could it be that God wants us to ask questions so that we can get to know him better?

I. THE LIFE OF JESUS

3. Arguments for God

AIM: To explore two of the traditional arguments for the existence of God.

EQUIPMENT NEEDED: Paper, felt-tip pens, a large number of 'Lego' pieces.

Introduction
So far the young people have thought about pictures of God and have asked questions about him. There is a range of traditional arguments for the existence of God and in this session two of those arguments will be investigated.

Activity
Invite the young people to pair off i.e. to choose a partner, and then sit back-to-back with that partner on the floor. One of the partners (A) is given ten pieces of Lego. He then passes them to the other partner (B) with instructions about how the pieces should be assembled. Partner B is not allowed to speak or to ask questions, nor may Partner A look at what B is doing. At the end of the exercise ask A to comment on how he expected the object to look and ask B to comment on how clear A's instructions were. Reverse roles and let the game run again.

This game illustrates very simply how difficult it is to use words clearly and to convey meaning. If it's that difficult to assemble only ten pieces of Lego is it any wonder that talk about God is so complex?

Bearing all this in mind, introduce the group to the notion that for centuries philosophers have been trying to find convincing and reasonable arguments for the existence of God – and amongst these arguments there are two which have been very popular.

(a) *The Cosmological Argument:* from Greek: 'Cosmos' = Universe
'Logos' = Word

Invite a member of the group to choose any object in the room and trace it back through time to its origins. Thus, for instance: suppose a china vase is selected:
The line of development would be (working backwards):
Vase – shop – wholesaler – manufacturer – quarries for China clay . . .
Draw a diagram to show the connections.

In that drawing the young people will have been hovering around the edges of a very ancient argument. It can be dated back to Aristotle, a Greek Philosopher who lived from 384-322 B.C. The essence of this argument is: Imagine you own the vase. Ask yourself the question: does the vase *need* to exist? It is quite reasonable to think that the vase need never have existed. The more you consider this argument the more it becomes clear that nothing *needs* to exist. "Ah", says the philosopher, "Is there anything in the world which really needs to exist?"

Everything that exists has a cause. There must be a First Cause i.e. someone or something which started it all off, and that First Cause *needs* to exist otherwise nothing could have come about.

That is the Cosmological Argument, an argument used by many to argue for God's existence. Like all such arguments it has its weaknesses. Encourage the group to discuss the argument and to see what they make of it.

Then try the second popular argument:

(b) *The Teleological Argument:* from Greek: 'Telos' = Purpose
'Logos' = Word

It goes like this: Imagine you had never seen a watch before and that you were to find one lying on the ground. By looking at it you might conclude that it was designed for a *purpose*, and if so, that there must be a designer (in the same way that your 'Lego' toy had a designer).

The problem with this argument is this. If you look at, for example, a bird, you can see that when it sits on a branch its claws 'lock' in such a way that it cannot fall off. So far so good, and before Darwin and his theory of evolution you might have said: "and so that proves that God designed the bird". But you know that the reason the bird can't fall off the branch is not because it was *designed* not to, but because through evolution that was the most successful pattern i.e. those birds which 'fell off', as it were, did not survive.

That, of course, is a gross over-simplification of the evolutionary hypothesis. It has been well argued, for instance, that 'randomness' and 'chance' would be necessary features of a Creator's plans. The argument remains powerful. The universe as we know it seems to be orderly and to have pattern – what better way of explaining this than by saying there must be a God? You might also ask the question: "Why does the universe exist at all?"

Again, allow plenty of free-ranging discussion of this philosophical argument.

(*Note:* One of the problems facing us as teachers is that not only do young people have little knowledge of Christianity, they have equally scanty knowledge of the current state of scientific thought. If you have a scientist in the parish who would be willing to come along to join in the discussion of these arguments that could be very helpful, not least in dispelling some of the over-simple views of science which people hold.)

Conclusion
The two arguments here put forward for the existence of God are both helpful and enjoyable, but in themselves they cannot prove that God exists. They are more like signposts than anything else, that is, they point us in the right sort of direction.

So – how can we know God?

We shall be looking at this question in the next session . . . .

I. THE LIFE OF JESUS

4. Knowledge of God

AIM: To help the participants think about the ways in which we know God.

EQUIPMENT NEEDED:
1 A carrier bag complete with ten or twelve items which can be used for a guess-the-object game.
2 A carrier bag complete with six or eight items which can be used for a guess-the-smell game.
3 An unusual object which can be used for a guess-the-purpose-of-this-object game.
4 Notebook and pencil.

Introduction
In the last session we were looking at two of the popular arguments for the existence of God. In this session we are going to be looking at ways of knowing God.

Activity
Without the young people watching place ten or twelve objects of different shapes and sizes in a plastic bag (none of them must be sharp, unpleasant or dangerous). Tie up the top of the plastic bag leaving just enough room for a hand and arm to be inserted. Ask each of the participants in turn to place their hands in the bag – and simply from the feel of the objects to guess what they are. Each participant must write their answers on a sheet of paper. At the end of the game invite each person to reveal what they have written. Then open the bag and show everyone what the objects were. Compare the guesses with the real things.

Afterwards discuss how they each used their sense of touch to try to ascertain what the object was. What part did imagination play? What other skills e.g. of deduction, did they use?

Then try another game, this time using the sense of smell. Ask each person in the group to close their eyes. Then provide six or eight different containers each having a distinctive smell e.g. after-shave, perfume, ointment, nutmeg. Pass the containers from person to person asking each to smell the contents and then to try to identify it.

After the activity discuss how, as in the sense of touch, when only using one sense (in this case, smell) they nevertheless were able to make some good deductions about each object.

Discuss afterwards the importance of our senses in helping us to understand our world.

Bring out that, so far, making sense has been reasonably straightforward. Now place in front of the group a highly unusual object. You ask them simply by looking at it (don't use touch or smell or taste or hearing), to try to discover what it is. They have to guess its origin and purpose. (Could a local antique shop lend you an object for this game if you can think of nothing yourself?)

Mid-way conclusion
The senses of touch and smell and sight, taste and hearing are used by humans to make sense (note the play on words) of the world, but they can only be useful when the mind co-ordinates the material and makes a pattern of it. (You could play a game in which by looking at random splodges of paint on a piece of paper you attempt to see a pattern, cf. seeing patterns and shapes in clouds, cf. the 'Man in the Moon'.)

But, there is no way in which we can come to know God through our five senses, at least, not directly.

So: discuss
How do people come to know God? There are at least five ways of knowing God:

Prayer: As we pray we meet God, who communicates with us at the deepest levels of our personalities. Prayer is a natural and universal human activity, a way in which every individual and God can focus on each other.

Thinking: Prayer and thinking are very closely linked, both, for example, use words: both try to put into words the deepest feelings we have. If you picture yourself like an inverted cone of rock – the layers with your deepest feelings come right at the base, then just above them comes the layer of prayer and, fading imperceptibly into it, the layer of thinking. As we think carefully about things we get in touch with the layers of ourselves and, ultimately, in touch with God who is, as it were, the spring bubbling up through all the fissures in the layers bringing life and vivacity.

Other people: Jesus made it very plain that God is at the heart of people's needs. ("I was in prison and you visited me . . . hungry and you fed me . . .") As we get to know people well we shall see in them aspects of God. Some people, the saints, seem to be

	like stained-glass through which the Light of God shines brilliantly.
The Bible:	The Bible has been for millions of people over hundreds of years the gateway to God. In reading it, in study and in meditation, they have found that God speaks to them through its words.
The Sacraments:	Although God is actively present everywhere, there seem to be special events in which his activity comes to a clear focus. Amongst these are the sacraments of Baptism and Holy Communion. They are places where God discloses himself to us.

. . . which brings us to the most important point of all. Both the Bible and the Church have taught that we can know God because, as Love, he chooses to reveal himself to us – and reveals himself as he really is in Jesus of Nazareth.

I. THE LIFE OF JESUS

5. Putting a face on God: Jesus

AIMS: To introduce the gospel of Mark.
To begin a portrait of Jesus.

EQUIPMENT NEEDED:
1 Sixteen or more stories cut from a local newspaper including adverts, photographs.
2 Writing paper and pencils.
3 A painting of Jesus.

Introduction
The four previous sessions have been exploring the idea of "God", now the time has come to focus attention on Jesus who, as a child once said, "put a face on God".

Activity
1 Scatter the newspaper stories in random order on a large flat surface where everyone can see them e.g. on a carpet or table. Then ask the group to arrange them in order, beginning with the story they find *most* important, and ending with the story they find *least* important.
  Discuss the reasons lying behind the choice.
2 Rearrange the stories so that they have a random pattern again. One of the group is asked to be 'editor' i.e. to arrange them so that there is an important and eye-catching story at the beginning, an eye-catching story in the middle and an eye-catching story at the end.
  Discuss the reasons for the choice.
3 Rearrange the stories so that they have a random pattern again. Another member of the group is asked to arrange them as in 2 above. Repeat this exercise twice.
  Discuss how, with a limited amount of material from which to choose, each 'editor' emphasises different aspects. Does 'personality' affect the arrangement?

Now turn to Mark's gospel:
Look carefully at the opening sentences of chapter 1.

Look carefully at the final chapter and, in particular, chapter 16 verses 1-8. (That was the place at which the most ancient manuscripts agree that Mark finished his Gospel: see later note.)

Look carefully at Mark 8 verses 27-30. These three passages are the equivalent of the eye-catching opening, middle and end of exercise 2 and 3 above.

One of the things you are trying to help the young people understand is that we see Jesus through the spectacles of Mark as writer and editor. It isn't as though Jesus wrote his own life-story and we could read that directly. All that we have, and it is of course more than adequate, are the portraits of Jesus given to us by Mark, Matthew, Luke and John.

At which point someone in the group is bound to say: "How do we know that Jesus really existed? Perhaps it's all made up." It's a question to which we need to give serious attention. There are two major blocks of evidence to show that Jesus really did exist:
(a) the New Testament
(b) other historical material.
Ignore the New Testament for the moment and look at the other evidence.

Tacitus, a Roman historian who lived *c*. A.D.56-116, writing about the burning of Rome in A.D.64 said "Nero fastened the guilt and inflicted the most exquisite tortures on a class hated for their abominations, called Christians by the populace. Christus, from whom the name had its origin, suffered the extreme penalty during the reign of Tiberius at the hands of one of our procurators: Pontius Pilate."

A Jewish historian, Josephus (born A.D.38), not at all in sympathy with Christianity wrote in his Jewish history *Antiquities of the Jews*, the following: "Ananias . . . assembled the Sanhedrin and brought before them James the brother of Jesus, who was called Christ."

Then there is another Roman historian, Suetonius. He was private secretary to the Emperor, Hadrian, and in one of his *Lives of the Caesars*, in fact in the 'Life of Claudius', he writes: "Since the Jews constantly made disturbances at the instigation of Chrestus he expelled them from Rome."

These are three pieces of reasonably objective evidence from non-believers about the existence of Jesus. And that, plus all the books of the New Testament, must surely be convincing enough. It's much more than we have for many other figures in history.

★ ★ ★ ★ ★

We may be certain then that Jesus of Nazareth existed – but what was he like? The answer is, we don't know. Trevor Shannon in his book *Jesus* puts it very clearly:

"Jesus was a Jew from the Middle East. He was a member of what we call the Semitic races. He is therefore likely to have been dark-skinned, looking perhaps like a Palestinian Arab today."

If he were of average height for a man of the time he would have been 5 foot 6 inches or 5 foot 7 inches tall. We know that men were generally smaller in those days, partly from the evidence of clothes and skeletons. Also, a mile was measured by the Roman army to be 1000 double paces. 'Mile' actually means 'a thousand'. A modern man of average height would walk a mile in about 900 double paces, or, to put it more simply, in about 1800 strides.

Clement of Alexandria (A.D. 155-215) said that Jesus was 'ugly'.

Origen of Alexandria (A.D. 185-254) quoted Isaiah 53:2-3 to refer to Jesus. The verses say:

> 'He had no beauty, no majesty to draw our eyes,
>   no grace to make us delight in him;
> his form, disfigured, lost all the likeness of a man,
>   tormented and humbled by suffering;
>   we despised him, we held him of no account,
>   a thing from which men turn away their eyes.'

Tertullian (A.D. 160-220) said that Jesus resembled 'a wretched little boy'."

Ask the group to compare that with the portraits of Jesus they may know. (Have a look at the stained-glass windows in your local church and in an illustrated New Testament.) What particular characteristics are the artists attempting to convey?

★ ★ ★ ★ ★

Although we cannot know the physical characteristics of Jesus, and although we have to a certain extent to see him through the spectacles of others, we can imagine the kind of person he might have been – and that will be the subject of the next session . . . .

I. THE LIFE OF JESUS

6. A day in the life

AIM: To see what a typical day in Jesus' life might have been like.

EQUIPMENT NEEDED: Felt-tip pens, drawing paper, tape-recorder.

Introduction
In the previous session we established that Jesus of Nazareth really existed and we saw that we could get to know about him through the portrait composed by Mark. That theme is continued in this session.

A thumb-nail sketch
Ask the group to pair-off. Each person has a sheet of paper and a pen. On the paper they are asked to draw four symbols which will give clues about the character of their partner. For example, if 'A' likes pop music 'B' would draw a symbol for that on his paper. If 'B' likes sport 'A' would draw a suitable symbol. When the exercise is finished ask each pair to describe their symbols and say why they have chosen them. Allow time to discuss how accurate the symbols are and whether or not they provide a complete portrait of the person concerned.

Then look up the following Biblical passages: Mark 1:16-18; Mark 3:1-6; Mark 6:30-34; Mark 4:1-9, and for each quotation ask the young people to draw an appropriate symbol to show the kind of person Jesus was. Compare the symbols one with another and discuss the differences and the similarities. Help the group to compose a composite set of symbols to illustrate what they as a group think Jesus was like.

A day in the life
Another way of trying to discover what makes a person tick is to find out how they spend their time. Many newspapers and magazines run articles with some such title as 'A Day in the Life . . .'.

Activity
Invite one person to be an interviewer and someone else to do the interviewing – and with the tape-recorder make a very brief programme entitled "A Day in the Life . . .". You could, if you wished, have two interviews, one indicating a typical working-day and the other a leisure-day. When the tape-recording is finished discuss the similarities and differences.

A DAY IN THE LIFE

A 'typical day' tells us quite a lot about the person concerned. In St Mark's Gospel there is an account of a day in the life of Jesus. Look at Mark 1, verses 21-39. Read the passage carefully.

Background information
A *synagogue* was the religious meeting place of the town. The primary functions of a synagogue were prayer and study. It may be that in the period when the Temple still stood, a synagogue could well have been nothing more than a large meeting room in a private house or part of a larger structure set aside for worship. Archaeologically there is no evidence for synagogues before the middle of the third century A.D., but traditionally it has been assumed that synagogues were large oblong buildings in which the scrolls of the Law had pride of place. Men sat separately from the women and children. (See *Archaeology, The Rabbis and Early Christianity:* Meyers and Strange, S.C.M.)

Capernaum ("the village of Nahum") was a town of about 300,000 square metres, with a population of between 12,000 and 15,000. The town was laid out in regular blocks of one-storey houses – each block was about 40 metres x 40 metres. Each house would contain a group of rooms around a courtyard where the ovens stood. Outside staircases led to flat roofs – normally constructed of beams, branches, rushes and mud. Although no archaeological remains of the synagogue have been found (see Mark 1:21), we may imagine that it would be a simple building about 7½ metres x 8½ metres, with columns inside to hold up the roof. There would probably be benches on three sides.

The major industries of Capernaum were agriculture and fishing.

The evil Spirit   The Sabbath (the Jewish holy day – Saturday) opens with Jesus teaching in the synagogue (there was no officiating minister at a synagogue, so any male could be asked to preach). The people were amazed at his teaching, and then he is confronted by a man 'possessed by an evil spirit'.

At the time of Jesus it was believed that people could be possessed by spiritual powers. The man screamed at Jesus: 'I know who you are.' Note that this was a very powerful thing to say. To know someone's name was to know their real nature and thus to have power over them. Jesus heals the man simply by speaking, and the people are amazed.

They see that the power of his teaching and his healing are immense. The forces of the 'devil' are hostile to God and thus in having power over them Jesus is saying that God's Kingdom is breaking in.

Discuss this healing. We may no longer believe in evil spirits – but do we think that Jesus has the power to bring peace to damaged lives?

THE LIFE OF JESUS

The healing of Simon's mother-in-law   In this healing Jesus does not say anything, he simply touches Simon's mother-in-law and she gets better.

The crowds come for healing   After sunset (the Jews reckoned their days from sunset to sunset, and therefore this was after the Sabbath) the crowds come flocking to Jesus and he heals those who are ill.

Jesus needs to be alone   Following the demands of the day before, it is not surprising that Jesus wants to be alone and to pray. Even then he is not left in peace, Simon and the others come looking for him and Jesus says that he must travel around the area telling people of the coming of God's Kingdom.

There are so many questions raised for discussion in this passage that it may be difficult to decide which is most appropriate for the group. There will be opportunities in later sessions to discuss 'evil spirits', and 'healing' and prayer. The central point is that this was a typical day in Jesus' life. To keep that in mind, if you have time, you could ask one of the group to imagine himself/herself as a disciple and to describe the day from his/her point of view.

I. THE LIFE OF JESUS

7. Stepping in the shoes

AIM: To enable the participants to step into the shoes of a Gospel event.

EQUIPMENT NEEDED: Bible. Space in which to develop role plays.

Introduction
From the 'Day in the life' session the young people should have begun to see what life was like for Jesus, the disciples, and those with whom they came into contact. It takes only a little imagination to get deeper into the stories and to experience some of the emotional content of what was going on.

Bible study
Invite the young people to read Mark 2:1-12, slowly and carefully. When they have finished ask them with which of the characters they most identified: was it Jesus? the paralysed man? the friends? the house-owner? the lawyers? the crowd? Ask them to read the story again and, when they have done so, explain that you are going to interview them as though they were the character in the story and not themselves. It is your task as the interviewer to discover from each person in the group how they saw the miracle. For example, the interviewer might ask the paralysed man: How long had you been ill? What caused your illness? Who made the decision to take you to Jesus? What did it feel like when you were being carried up on to the roof?

Obviously, the interview needs to be conducted sensitively and in a way which encourages the imagination of those being interviewed. It's impossible to predict beforehand what the interview will reveal. You will have to be quick on your mental feet and ask questions which require more than 'Yes' or 'No' answers. You will find as the interviews progress and you become more and more drawn into the humanness of the story that both your enjoyment and the insight of the young people will deepen. It reminds us that it was ordinary people like ourselves who met Jesus and who were transformed by the meeting.

The interviews could last for most of the lesson so do make sure that there is time to stand back from the role plays and discuss what each person has learnt from them before concluding.

The Bible study inevitably raises the question of healing, a complex but interesting subject, and one which you will need to tackle with openness and care. There are, of course, many accounts in the Gospels of Jesus' healing gifts. It would seem that he was concerned for the whole person, body, mind and spirit, hence, in this story, the question about forgiveness. It would be wrong to assume that illness is either a divine punishment for sin or a direct result of sin, though the latter can be true. A very heavy smoker, for example, can bring an illness on himself through his addiction. What the Christian believes is that God is on the side of healing and wholeness and longs for mankind to be whole.

Because this subject is so difficult you might like to invite to the group a local doctor or health visitor or clergyman to hear their views about the nature of healing, although this could be left to the next session when the subject of healing will be looked at again.

I. THE LIFE OF JESUS

8. Jesus the healer

AIM: To come to some understanding of the work of Jesus as a healer.

EQUIPMENT NEEDED: Record player, record ('Sea Interludes', Benjamin Britten), paper and pen, Bible.

Introduction
The last session inevitably raised questions about the nature of healing. Those questions are pursued in this session.

'You make me sick'/'On top of the world'
There are any number of everyday comments which we use almost without thinking. When we are very happy we might describe ourselves as 'feeling great'; 'on top of the world'; 'happy as Larry'; 'on song'; 'on top form'; 'firing on all four cylinders'. And when we're unhappy we have similar phrases: 'I feel rotten'; 'down in the dumps'; 'blue'; 'fed up'; 'sick to death'.

Ask the group to write on one large sheet of paper all the phrases they know describing well-being; and on another large sheet of paper all those phrases which describe real unhappiness. Compare the two lists and help them to think about the relationship between how we feel and how we are. There is an intimate and profound link between body, mind and soul. 'Health' does not simply mean physical health. Discuss with them what they believe 'health' is, and write those findings on a large sheet of paper for all to see.

In Mark's Gospel there is a clever editorial passage in which he puts two stories about peace side-by-side. The first: Mark 4:35-41 is about peace in the natural world, and the second: Mark 5:1-20, about inner peace. You could explore this theme in this way.

Activity
Play the 'Storm' sequence from Britten's 'Sea Interludes': the group will need to listen to the music in silence. At the end of the music each member of the group should write an outline of a story/poem for which the music has given him or her ideas.

When the stories are completed listen to the music again and afterwards each member of the group reads aloud their outline story.

The storm music fits the story of the stilling of the storm perfectly: Mark 4:35-41. Read aloud this passage and listen to the music again if you so wish.

Note
There are three ideas which underlie the story of the stilling of the storm:
1 The sea or a great storm was understood by the Jews as a symbol of chaos and evil, from which only God's power could save them. (See Psalm 69:1-2, 14-15).
2 The ability to control the sea was considered a characteristic of divine power: see Psalm 89:8-9.
3 The person with supreme confidence in God will never doubt God's ability to save: see Psalm 46:1-3.

The story of the stilling of the storm can be understood symbolically. We are not in a position to determine the historical 'truth' of the event.

Activity
Discuss the 'stilling of the storm' story, then listen to the music and note how the violence and fury of the story is resolved into some moments of tranquillity.

Ask the group to look again at their original stories and to try to resolve the story so that chaos is brought towards order, the furious towards peace, the violence towards tranquillity, and then, when the stories are completed, read them aloud.

Activity
Read Mark 5:1-20: Jesus brings peace to a chaotic and tormented man. As we can see, Mark deliberately edited his Gospel so that these two stories of Jesus bringing peace were next to each other. In the first he brings peace to 'nature' and in the second to a 'man' or, rather, in both, he brings order where there was once chaos.

Discuss (1) the story of 'Legion' and think especially of Jesus' power in bringing 'healing'.
(2) Does God bring order from chaos today?

I. THE LIFE OF JESUS

9. The Transfiguration of Jesus

AIM: To explore the story of the Transfiguration.

EQUIPMENT NEEDED: Paper, pens, Bible, sheet music, electric lamp, materials for stained-glass windows.

Introduction
The disciples' view of Jesus was transformed by their experience of his authority over chaos, yet there came a time when Jesus himself apparently underwent an experience of profound closeness to God which was later described as 'The Transfiguration'.

Activities
1 Invite each person in the group to solve a mathematical puzzle: e.g. If Tom has eleven sweets more than John, and John has four sweets more than Bill, and Bill only has two sweets, how many sweets does Tom have?
2 Invite each member of the group to look at a sheet of music. Ask all those who are able to read the music to sing the tune on it.
3 Ask each of the group to draw on a sheet of paper a design which could be the basis for a tapestry.

At the end of the three games, explain that each of the games is about a kind of transformation. In the maths game, words are transformed into numbers; in the music game, notation is transformed into sound; in the drawing game, the idea in the artist's head has been transformed onto paper. When the games are completed, discuss other examples of 'transformation' e.g. in engineering; architecture etc. Then read: Mark 9:1-9.

Note
There are several possible explanations of the Transfiguration story.
1 The events happened as described.
2 That this was a post-Resurrection appearance placed by Mark in the wrong context.
3 That the shining goodness you can see in some people was magnified in Christ.
4 That in some instances mystics at prayer have become, as it were, radiant with holiness.

You will know that Elijah is meant to represent the Prophets and Moses the Law. The cloud is a reference back to the Old Testament and to descriptions of God's glory.

When the reading is completed discuss which of those four possible explanations you find most credible. What are the advantages and disadvantages of each explanation?

Suppose that there is a sceptic in the group who thinks that nothing of the kind happened. You might ask the classic question: What kind of man must Jesus have been to have such stories told about him?

It could be that the Transfiguration is a poetic way of saying that the disciples saw the potential of Jesus. They could see his glory but not understand its meaning. For example you can see an electric light bulb and it is nothing – though it has potential – and only when connected is the potential realised. That example is a bit trite, but it may help.

Rather than be trapped into a "Did it happen or not?" argument, an argument which cannot be resolved, move the discussion on by trying to find ways in which people have described the glory of God. What would a good twentieth century picture of glory be? Ask the young people for their views. Help them to see that "reductionism" is not the only way of looking at the world:

> 'A sunset is only refraction of light.'
> 'Birdsong is only territory mechanism.'

Both of these descriptions are partly true but not the whole truth.

> 'A man that looks on glasse
> On it may stay his eye
> Or if he pleases through it passe
> And there the heavens espye.'
> George Herbert

If they are not convinced by your explanation try suggesting that their love-letters are only squiggles of ink on paper – a series of random jots and blobs – and they will begin to appreciate that there is more to life than "Reductionism".

There is no way in which the story of the Transfiguration can be neatly packaged, absorbed and understood. It is indeed bewildering and baffling, but a reminder, if such a one were needed, that Christianity is also concerned with holiness and mystery, with awe and wonder.

I. THE LIFE OF JESUS

10. Jesus the story-teller

AIM: To appreciate the skills and the content of Jesus' story-telling.

EQUIPMENT NEEDED: Bible, paper, pens, tape-recorder.

Introduction
Over-familiarity with some of Jesus' stories may have blunted the edge of our appreciation. There is no doubt, however, that he was an extraordinarily gifted story-teller and presumably chose this medium for his teaching as being the most effective possible.

Activity
Invite each person in the group to tell a true story about something good, exciting or frightening which has happened to them. When the stories are complete discuss how important the first-hand experience of the story-teller was.

Then look at Mark 4:1-9 and read it aloud. Afterwards, consider these questions:
1 What first-hand experience might Jesus have been drawing on?
2 Where did Jesus teach?
3 Who did he teach?
4 What was the point of the story?
5 What relevance does the story have for us?

Ask each member of the class to count the number of words Jesus used in that story, the story of the Sower, and then suggest that they try to write a story with a beginning, a middle and an end, using exactly the same number of words. Having done this discuss your conclusions about Jesus' skills as a story-teller, and then ask why Jesus used stories for his teaching. There were at least three reasons:
1 Stories are memorable.
2 They capture the imagination.
3 Because they are open-ended they force the listener to think for himself and to come to a decision.

* * * * *

But Jesus did not use only stories for his teaching. Following in a long and ancient Old Testament tradition, he also used 'parables' in which drama was involved to heighten the impact.

Read John 13:1-17. What was Jesus conveying to his disciples through this dramatic parable?

Read Mark 11:1-11: another acted parable. Discuss what effect such an incident might have had on the local populace.

Activity
If your church invited this group to create an acted parable for use in worship, what would be created?

I. THE LIFE OF JESUS

11. The beginning of the end

AIM: To appreciate the sequence and meaning of Jesus' last days.

EQUIPMENT NEEDED: Bible; candle; paper and felt-tip pens; supply of colour magazines.

Introduction
If you look carefully at the Gospels you will see that the last week of Jesus' life takes up a very large part of the narrative. It was, and is, the most significant week of his life because in it we can glimpse the depths of God's love, Jesus' self-emptying, his solidarity with mankind.

The session
So far in this course the sessions have been activity-based. There may well be something to be said for a complete change at this stage. Often young people only have a sense of Jesus' life as episodic i.e. they know some of his parables, some of his miracles, but they may not have any sense of the sweep of the story. Instead of an activity, therefore, explain that you are going to read aloud to them, and that all you expect them to do is to be attentive and simply listen. In many Rudolf Steiner schools when stories are told the narrator lights a single candle and sits next to it. It's a technique worth copying for it gives the young people something to look at as you read and provides a focus for their imaginations.

Set the scene
Jesus was born thirty-three years ago to a young woman, Mary. He grew up in the relative obscurity of a small village in Galilee; no doubt he attended synagogue; helped his father in his carpentry business, played with or looked after the younger members of his family. For thirty years his life was like anyone else's, then one day it changed. He went off to see John the Baptist – and his awareness of his own profound relationship with God deepened and deepened. He taught; he healed. He gathered around him a group of disciples and proclaimed the coming of God's Kingdom. For three years he lived as a wandering prophet and story-teller, a man much loved by the people and much misunderstood by them. He challenged some of the central teachings of the Jewish faith; he put loyalty to God's love above loyalty to God's law. He inevitably clashed with both the political and religious leaders of his day, and they believed that for the sake of religious and political stability he was a problem to which a solution had to be found. Jesus, meanwhile, had realised that God's way was not the way of power,

but the way of suffering. He felt that he had to follow that way no matter where it led . . . .

The turning point comes at Mark 10:32. Mark expresses it in great economy of style: "They were on the road going up to Jerusalem, Jesus leading the way, and the disciples were filled with awe; while those who were behind were afraid."

And from that moment on the battle lines are drawn. First, he has to show his disciples yet again what God's way was like: *Read Mark 10:32-45*.

Then, in the heart of the Jewish capital, Jerusalem, he challenges the central beliefs of the Jewish religion: *Read Mark 11:15-19*.

This causes confusion because the leaders are baffled by the nature of his authority: *Read Mark 11:27b-33*.

Two of the major religious groupings, the Pharisees and the Sadducees, try to trap him with questions (note that the politicians, 'the men of Herod's party', are also lurking there): *Read Mark 12:13-27*.

A lawyer, either in all innocence or in order to score a point, asks him for his opinion 'Which commandment is first of all?' *Read Mark 12:28-34*.

So the stage is set for the final conflict . . .

Activity
Allow much time for discussion of the way the Gospel narrative unfolds . . . the steady progression towards the climax; the sense of impending tragedy; the encapsulation of the challenge in those five episodes.

Divide the group, if it's large enough, into five. Ask each group to look at one of the episodes just recounted and either through drawing a symbol or through creating a collage (using cut-up colour magazine pictures) to illustrate the heart of each episode. At the end discuss with each of the five what they have done and, if possible, mount the drawings or collages as a sequence like a Way of the Cross.

I. THE LIFE OF JESUS

12. The last days

AIM: To appreciate the sequence and meaning of Jesus' last days.

EQUIPMENT NEEDED: Bible; candle; drawing paper and pens.

Introduction
The last session, with its five insistent drum-beats, began to reveal the inevitable discords of the last days. Continue the theme. Recap the previous theme by referring to the five-fold challenge. Explain that you are going to continue to read aloud to them . . . . Begin at Mark 14:1, and continue until 16:8.

At the end of the reading ask the young people to sit in silence for a couple of minutes, and reflect on the way the story unfolded. Suggest that there will be one image from the story which they will find will keep coming back to them – and whatever that is (it will be different for each one), ask them to think deeply about that image. At the end of two minutes ask each of them to say what their image was, and to draw it on a large sheet of paper. Try then to put those images in sequence, to continue the five-fold series built up in the previous lesson. If it is felt appropriate, their drawings (with an explanatory note) could be displayed in the church.

It is right that the young people should face the grim realities of the trial, the torture and the crucifixion itself – but don't let this become morbid. The Gospel-writers, you will note, are very sparing in the way they recount the event.

You will then need to take the youngsters through and beyond the death of Jesus to those strange and haunting words of Mark 16:1-8.

Scholars, in trying to understand the way Mark's Gospel ends, face a real problem. It can be stated like this:

1 The Gospel ends in an unusual way. The phrase 'They were afraid', is translated in the Jerusalem Bible as 'they were afraid . . .'. Note the punctuation.
2 Some questions:
    (a) Did Mark intend to end his Gospel in this way? 'Perhaps', say some scholars, 'he did so to show that all Christians now share in the elusive beauty of the resurrection. There's no need for Mark to say anymore.'
    (b) If Mark did not intend to end the Gospel like this what happened to the missing piece? Why couldn't he have been asked to supply it? Some, a little

tongue-in-cheek, have even suggested that Mark was arrested by anti-Christian forces in mid-sentence and thus the Gospel was never completed.

You will need to help the young people to think carefully about the resurrection and encourage them to discuss what they think might have happened. No doubt they will want to discuss all the unlikeliest possibilities, e.g. 'Jesus didn't die at all, he was only in a coma' – in which case what happened to him afterwards?; or 'Jesus and Barabbas swapped places at the last moment and Jesus did not die . . . ' – again would everyone have been taken in by this? or 'Jesus did die but his body was moved from the tomb by the disciples' – would they have proclaimed Jesus' resurrection with such zeal if they knew it to be false?

There are certain positive comments which can be made in favour of physical resurrection, i.e.

1 If Jesus' body was simply 'mouldering in the grave', why, when the disciples proclaimed the resurrection, was the body not produced?
2 Why, if it was a hoax, should the Gospel writers have insisted that the first witnesses were women when, in legal disputes of that time, a woman's testimony was considered worthless?
3 What must have happened to change the disciples from a bunch of terrified and bewildered men into a group bubbling with confidence and joy?
4 When their whole mental world-picture could not conceive of a crucified Messiah (not unlike us unable to conceive of a round square), how did they suddenly see the profound truth of the nature of God in Jesus the victim? Does not the resurrection event provide a clue for this change?

Of course, it's impossible to produce a knock-down argument for the historicity of a physical resurrection but, in spite of the difficulties involved, the Church has long taught and proclaimed that 'resurrection' is the answer which best meets all the questions.

But, the Church also says, the resurrection of Jesus is not simply an unusual event which took place two thousand years ago. It is a living and present reality to believers. The risen Jesus continues to make himself known to people today – through word, through sacrament, through personal encounters.

★ ★ ★ ★ ★

The first twelve sessions of the course have introduced us to the life of Christ. We now move on to explore the origins and life of the Church.

II. THE LIFE OF THE CHURCH

II. THE LIFE OF THE CHURCH

1. The Holy Spirit

AIM: To explore the biblical images of the Holy Spirit.

EQUIPMENT NEEDED: Candle and matches; Bible; prayer book; *Lord of the Flies* by William Golding; *In Hazard* (Penguin) by Richard Hughes; pens and paper.

Introduction
The words 'Holy Spirit' are puzzling to our modern ears. They are used, of course, with great frequency in worship – in hymns, in creeds and in biblical material. The Church believes that the Holy Spirit is one of the three 'persons' of the God-head: Father, Son and Holy Spirit. In this session, we shall be exploring the symbols of the Holy Spirit in order to come to a closer understanding.

Fire
Activity
Place a candle in the centre of the room, light it and ask the young people to look at the candle flame in silence for one minute. At the end of the minute write on a sheet of paper the words which best describe the flame. Then ask each person to observe the candle very, very closely and to draw on a sheet of paper a picture of that candle. Having done that, then read to the group the account from *Lord of the Flies* of the forest fire, and ask each of them afterwards to write a short story entitled 'Flame'.

Discuss their stories with them.

Read Acts 2:1-4 and, in the light of all that they have learnt about fire as a symbol, discuss why 'fire' was chosen as a description of the Holy Spirit.

Read Acts 2:1-4 again and invite the group to answer the following questions:
1 What do you think those first Christians felt like?
2 If you had been present what would you have seen, if anything?

Dove
Introduction
The dove is a universal emblem of peace but no one is entirely certain why the dove was considered as a symbol for the Holy Spirit. It may refer back to the

opening chapters of Genesis where God is pictured like a huge bird hovering over the waters of chaos. It undoubtedly has echoes of the Noah's ark story i.e. a sign of God keeping his promise. It may be simply because a dove is such a beautiful creature . . .

Activity
If possible show the group a copy of the painting of a dove by Picasso, and discuss its qualities of lightness, purity and peace. Or, failing that, find in a bird book a picture of a dove and ask the young people to compose a list of words to describe it. Then, as with the 'Fire' sequence, using those words create a short story.

Wind
Introduction
The third great symbol of the Holy Spirit is the 'breath of God', that which God breathes into every creature to give it life (see Genesis 2:7).

Activity
Make a toy wind-mill with paper; or make paper aeroplane-darts; or, if the weather's suitable, make a kite and fly it. If you live in a town you could go on a town-trail and look for weather-vanes.

Discuss with the young people variations in wind-speed. Compare the gentleness of a summer breeze with the roughness of a winter storm. Read Richard Hughes' description of a storm in *In Hazard* (Penguin).

Discuss why the early Church used 'wind' as a symbol for God's Holy Spirit. Look up a Whitsun hymn and see how poets have continued the breath/wind theme . . .

Conclusion
Those three symbols of Fire, the Dove and Wind have at least the idea of 'energy' in common. None of the symbols are static. Quite the reverse. The early Christians were obviously changed dramatically and radically by the Pentecost experience. But the Church does not believe that that was a one-off event. It believes that the Holy Spirit continues to be active and at work amongst Christians today, bringing gifts to them and to the Church as a whole. It sees the Holy Spirit as bringing the Church into being, sustaining and guiding it in the way it should go.

Invite the young people to look at this collect for Pentecost and discuss what they think it means and the implications it has for them and their church.

Almighty God
who on the day of Pentecost
sent your Holy Spirit to the disciples
with the wind from heaven and in tongues of flame,
filling them with joy
   and boldness to preach the Gospel:
send us out in the power of the same Spirit
to witness to your truth
and to draw all men to the fire of your love;
through Jesus Christ our Lord.
      (Second Collect for Pentecost, *A.S.B. 1980*)

They could either learn that prayer off-by-heart or, if you prefer, the *Book of Common Prayer* collect for Whitsunday or the prayer used in your church; you could use these collects to conclude the session.

II. THE LIFE OF THE CHURCH

2. How the Church began

AIM: To be aware of the beginning of the Church's life.

EQUIPMENT NEEDED: Bible; clock; chalice; paper and pens.

Introduction
Young people often find it difficult to visualise the sweep of history. The younger they are the more impossible it is. Nelson becomes mixed up with the Pharoahs, and Henry VIII with the Romans. Nevertheless they are interested in ancient artefacts and, if the subject is approached enthusiastically and with imagination, can gain a real understanding of their own Christian roots.

Activity
In the middle of the room on a table place the chalice used by your church for Holy Communion. Next to it place an unwound clock. Explain that you are going to attempt to travel back through time. Move the clock hands one hour backwards. What was anyone doing one hour ago? Move the hands back twelve hours. What was happening then? Twenty-four hours?

Give up using the clock as your visual aid and go back rapidly through the years, five years ago; ten years ago, and stop when you have got to a time prior to their birth. Now move attention to the chalice used by the church every week; last week; the week before that; five years before that; ten years ago. . . . That chalice was being used by the people of the church before the confirmation candidates were born. . . . Now use it to travel back through time – World War II; World War I; the Victorian era; the French Revolution . . . back as far as the chalice will take you. Get the story to the imaginative point where the chalice was only a lump of iron/silver in a hillside . . . take that as your next vehicle for time-travel. It was there in 1066 . . . when Alfred burnt the cakes . . . when the Romans invaded England . . . when Christ lived and walked the earth.

In other words, you have focussed the time-travel on an 'object' and this may help the group to visualise their link with the past.

Now, equally rapidly get them to trace their Christian family-tree. Who first told them about Jesus? Where did that person hear it from? Back and back to the point at which someone planted the local church (probably unknown), back in time to the first and unknown Christians crossing the sea to this country – as merchants? soldiers? traders? Trace the family descent, the way the Christian story has been passed from one generation to another until it gets back to the point at which Jesus calls his disciples.

Read: Mark 1:16-20 and Mark 3:13-18.

It could be said that the Church began when that first call was heard. But it could also be said that the Church began only after Jesus' death. Read Acts 2:1-13, and remind the group of their lesson about the 'Holy Spirit'. Then explain that Luke in the Acts of the Apostles gives a brief summary of how the very first Christians lived.

Read: Acts 2:42-47.

Compare those four activities in verse 42; 'to hear the Apostles teach; to share the common life; to break bread; to pray' with the way the local church lives. What remains the same after two thousand years? What has changed?

★ ★ ★ ★ ★

If the church you attend is very old, invite someone who knows its history to come to the group and briefly give a potted history of it. Or, if your church was built recently, invite someone who remembers its being built to come and talk about that time. Remember that you are trying to establish the link between the Church now and the Church when it began. Or: if you live close enough to your cathedral take the group on a visit and ask one of the cathedral guides to introduce its history. (You will need to organise this well in advance.)

★ ★ ★ ★ ★

Ask each of the group to make a time-chart either of their own church or of their own 'Christian family-tree' to show the links between their beliefs now and the beginnings of the early Church.

II. THE LIFE OF THE CHURCH

3. The nature of the Bible

AIM: To understand the nature of the Bible as a library.

EQUIPMENT NEEDED: Bible; books for the Activity; paper and pens.

Introduction
It is often thought, but quite incorrectly, that the Bible came first and the Church second. In fact the Bible as we now have it grew directly out of the early life of the Church.

The word "Bible" has an interesting history in itself: "It is derived from the Phoenician city of Byblos, the principal exporter of papyrus. The word was drawn into the Greek language as 'biblos' and into Latin as 'biblia'." *Collins Dictionary of the Bible.*

The Bible is not just one book. It is a collection of books bound together, a library rather than a single volume.

* * * * *

Activity
Put out on the floor of the room where you meet a selection of twenty books – vary their kind e.g. some cookery books, some encyclopaedias, some D-I-Y manuals; some novels; and at least eight children's books of a roughly similar nature e.g. children's encyclopaedias, children's novels.

Ask each member of the group to classify the books i.e. to arrange them in an order which they think most appropriate. Discuss the reason for the order. Eventually ask for the books to be divided simply into two different blocks e.g. adults and children; or novels and reference. Discuss the reasons. Then ask each person present to look at a copy of the Bible and on a sheet of paper to write down the two major divisions of the Bible i.e. Old Testament and New Testament.

Note
In some Bibles there is a third section called The Apocrypha. The word Apocrypha means literally secret or hidden things. But it is used in the Bible to refer to those books included in the early Latin and Greek versions of Scripture but which were not admitted as 'canonical' by the Jews. The apocryphal books were in Greek and the Jews admitted into their 'canon' only books originally written in Hebrew.

THE NATURE OF THE BIBLE

The word 'canon', literally meaning 'measuring rod', is the word used to describe the collection of books which both the Jews and the Christians regard as definitive. They were the measure against which other books were judged.

The word 'Testament' can also be translated as 'Covenant'. It means a solemn and binding promise.

The word 'Gospel' comes from the Anglo-Saxon 'God-spell' – God-story. It is a translation of the Greek word 'Evangelian' – good news.

★ ★ ★ ★ ★

Having established the two (or three) major divisions of the Biblical library now ask them to write on a sheet of paper the names of the first five books of the Old Testament and the first five books of the New Testament.

To explore the idea of the Bible as a library you could use this quiz:

About the Old Testament:

1   Which book is called by a word which looks like 'leaving'?
2   In which book would you look for some wise sayings?
3   Which book has a name which seems mathematical?
4   In which book might you find the story of a whale?
5   In which book would you look for a hymn?
6   In which two books would you look to find some of the history of Israel's kings?
7   It looks like 'work' but is in fact a beautiful poem. Which book is it?
8   How many books are there in the Old Testament?
9   What are the first ten words of the Old Testament?

. . . and about the New Testament:

1   Which book is named after the people who live in Italy's capital city?
2   Which book has a name which could mean 'vision' or 'dream'?
3   Which is the shortest book in the New Testament?
4   Which is the shortest Gospel?
5   The name of a column and the name of a gulf. There are two books named after this place. What are they?
6   What is the name of the book which has 'Apostles' in the title?
7   What is the name of the book beginning with 'H'?
8   How many books are there in the New Testament?
9   What does the very last sentence of the New Testament say?

THE LIFE OF THE CHURCH

Answers
Old Testament
1. Exodus
2. Proverbs
3. Numbers
4. Jonah
5. Psalms
6. I and II Kings
7. Job
8. 39
9. 'In the beginning, God created the heavens and the earth.'

New Testament
1. Romans
2. Revelation
3. Philemon
4. Mark
5. Corinthians I & II
6. Acts
7. Hebrews
8. 27
9. 'The grace of the Lord Jesus be with all the saints, Amen.'

II. THE LIFE OF THE CHURCH

4. How the Bible came to us

AIM: To see in outline how the Bible has come to us.

EQUIPMENT NEEDED:
1. Bible; pen/pencil.
2. Materials for the Activity.

Introduction
Ask the group for any proverbs that they know (A rolling stone . . . etc.), and ask them how they came to know them. Then offer them a few examples of sayings which have passed into everyday speech but which have a Biblical origin e.g. 'a Job's comforter'; the 'gospel truth'; 'before the Ark'; 'a good Samaritan'; 'casting your pearls before swine'; 'cast your bread on the waters'.

Remind the group that the Bible has not only infiltrated everyday speech, it has been extraordinarily influential in the way our culture has developed. People have died so that we might have a copy of the Bible in our own language. It's been banned, burned, smuggled, given away; it's been read in prisons, hospitals, P.O.W. camps; in the bush; in high-rise flats. It has reached every corner of the globe.

Discuss how its importance is symbolised in your church; is it kept on a special lectern e.g. a brass eagle? Is it carried in processions?

The early history of the Bible
As a book it has had an extraordinary history. Very, very roughly it goes like this:

1. *The Old Testament*
   The actual *writing* of the books of the Old Testament took place over several centuries before the birth of Jesus, but the *collection* was only made 'canonical' (see the definition in the previous lesson) in about the last thirty years of the first century A.D. (A.D. 70-100). There is no great certainty about this but most scholars are agreed that that was the case.

2. *The New Testament*
   The actual *writing* of the books of the New Testament took place between approximately 50 A.D. and 100 A.D. – though again some scholars would make those outside dates earlier.

   The *collection* of the books was only made canonical (see the definition in the previous lesson) between the third and fourth centuries A.D. There was a great deal of debate about which books should be 'in' and which should be 'out' and so the process of decision took a long time before it settled down.

It is worth remembering *the sequence* of the writings too – it is not what you might expect. This is very roughly the sequence:

a	Jesus alive – and teaching and preaching	30 A.D.
b	Jesus' teaching transmitted by word of mouth and perhaps a few written records	30-50 A.D.
c	Paul's letters (Epistles) to the Churches	50-62 A.D.
d	The first Gospel: Mark	sometime after 60 A.D.
e	Luke – Acts	sometime after 70 A.D.
f	Matthew's Gospel	sometime after 70 A.D.
g	John's Gospel	sometime after 70 A.D.
h	Book of Revelation	between 80 and 90 A.D.
i	The letters of John	around 100 A.D. (or even as late as 130 A.D.)

And from then on the picture becomes even more confused. But let's try to establish some important names and dates to get an outline of how our Bible came to us.

How did the Bible come to us?
1 *Jerome* ?347-?420

What we have to remember is that in the years after Jesus' death there was no concensus about which books were or were not canonical. What is more the languages in which the Scriptures were written also added complications to the development of the Bible.

The original *Old Testament* books had been written in *Hebrew*, but at the time of Alexander the Great (about 300 years B.C.), they had been translated into *Greek* – the most commonly used language of the world at that time. The *New Testament* books were also written in *Greek* though Jesus and his disciples had spoken a form of Hebrew called *Aramaic*.

So, after the death of Jesus the early Christians had as their scriptures: a Greek Old Testament and a Greek 'New Testament', (or, at least, the beginnings of a New Testament). As time went on large numbers of books were produced claiming to have been written by the apostles (most of them were not); and some churches would have had one collection of sacred writings whilst other churches would have had another collection. Just to make the situation even more complicated Latin was beginning to oust Greek as the main language of the world, and so by the time we come to the fourth century A.D. the situation was very confused indeed. There was obviously a need for an authoritative and laid-down version of the Bible, one about which all could agree.

Pope Damasus approached a great scholar and translator called Jerome in 382 and asked him to prepare such a version. He quickly went to work. By 383 he had translated the four Gospels from Greek into Latin, taking meticulous care over his translation. Then in 384 when Pope Damasus died Jerome left for Bethlehem. There he lived in a monastery and for the next thirty-four years he continued his translation task. Jerome's translation of the Bible, known as the *Vulgate*, was the basis for the development of many Bible translations from then on. He had gone back to the Greek and the Hebrew, to the original sources. It was an enormous and painstaking work, but because Latin remained the common language of Europe for many centuries the *Vulgate* was enormously influential.

2 *Alfred the Great* 849-99
Although King Alfred, King of England in the ninth century, is known in popular mythology as the burner of cakes, he was in fact a wise king and an enlightened scholar. He translated portions of the Bible into Anglo-Saxon and incorporated these passages in his Laws.

3 *John Wycliffe* ?1330-1384
The work of translating the *Vulgate* into English was done by five Oxford scholars, under the leadership of John Wycliffe and with Nicholas of Hereford acting as principal assistant. The whole Bible in English was in circulation by the time of Wycliffe's death in 1384.

It should be remembered that all this translation and writing had to be done by hand, printing had not yet been invented.

The purpose of Wycliffe's work was to make the Bible available to all – not just to the educated and the clergy who could read Latin.

4 *Gutenberg* ?1398-1468 and *Caxton* ?1422-91
Around 1454, a German, Gutenberg used moveable type for printing and, twenty years later, in 1477, Caxton began printing in England.

5 *William Tyndale* ?1492-1536
The setting up of printing presses and the scholarly interest in the Bible meant that the control the Church could keep upon the believers was lessened. William Tyndale was a great scholar and he learnt Hebrew so that he could

translate the Bible directly from that language into English. Such were the dangers of the times that he had to have the books printed in Germany and then virtually smuggled into England. He had completed the New Testament by 1525 but the Church, under the leadership of Cardinal Wolsey, was so incensed by his work that in the old St Paul's Churchyard a fire was kindled on which New Testaments were burnt. And in 1536, Tyndale himself was strangled, then burned at Vilvorde in Belgium. It is said that his last words were 'Lord, open the King of England's eyes'.

From then on, via the work of other translators such as Miles Coverdale (1488-1568), (it is his version of the Psalms which is used in the Book of Common Prayer), the Bible became more and more accessible to the public. The most famous translation of the Bible, the Authorised Version or King James Version, took forty-seven scholars four years to complete (1607-1611), and this version of the Bible held sway in England and throughout the English-speaking world until the twentieth century.

In this century there have been dozens of translations, amongst them: New English Bible; Good News Bible; Jerusalem Bible.

Meanwhile the work of translating the Bible into other languages goes on. Now the Bible is available in over 1,760 languages and in many countries the work of translation and distribution is carried out by a society which specialises in that field: The Bible Society.

★ ★ ★ ★ ★

Activity
How can you make this great story come alive for the group?

Spread out on the floor a number of sheets of paper on which are written all the names of the books of the Old Testament. Let all those sheets of paper be of the same colour – say white. Now explain that the time is three hundred years before Jesus – and a group of translators have been asked to translate the Old Testament from Hebrew into Greek.

Move the imaginary clock forward to the time of Jesus: and point out that the only scriptures he and the disciples had available were those of the Old Testament. Then: mark the time of the Crucifixion and Resurrection by putting a cross on the floor. (Make sure that the Old Testament papers are scattered higgledy-piggledy everywhere.) Then, as if creating a chronological time chart put down on the floor sheets of paper, (use a different colour paper), in the following order: Paul's Epistles; Mark; Luke; Acts; Matthew; John; Book of Revelation; Letters of John – and add a few extra sheets, with additional names on e.g. 'Gospel of

HOW THE BIBLE CAME TO US

Thomas'. Once you have done that put the Old Testament books into order on one side of the Cross, and the New Testament books into order on the other side.

So, you now have the Old Testament in order, and the New Testament in order, though all the books are written in Greek, and on the New Testament side there is no decision yet about whether or not some books e.g. Revelation are 'in' or 'out'.

Explain that it's now towards the end of the fourth century and Jerome comes on to the scene to make accurate translations of the Bible from Greek into Latin. At the same time decisions are made as to what is to be included in the New Testament: Revelation is 'in'.

By the end of the fourth century then, there is a complete Latin Old Testament and Latin New Testament, and that's how it remained for centuries until Alfred the Great translated some of the Bible into Anglo-Saxon, and centuries later, in the fourteenth century, John Wycliffe translated the Bible from Latin into English. Continue the time-chart on from there using the characters of the session i.e. Gutenberg; Caxton; Tyndale; Coverdale, and end with the Bibles now used by your group.

Remind them of the languages the process has gone through: (Hebrew; Greek; Latin; Mediaeval English; Twentieth Century English) to get to them.

Remind them of the time-scale: two thousand years.

★ ★ ★ ★ ★

You might find it helpful to invite in a local representative of the Bible Society or the Bible Reading Fellowship to help with this session.

Or, instead of sheets of paper on the floor, you could use velcro-backed paper on a felt-board to create a time-chart.

Or, you could ask a small group of adults from your parish to prepare a time-chart to help the young people understand the sequence of events.

It's complicated because of the inter-twining of languages and time-scales and personalities, but what you are trying to convey is the sweep of history of the Bible's origins and development. Not easy – but well worth a try.

II. THE LIFE OF THE CHURCH

5. The Old Testament

AIM: To grasp the sweep of Old Testament history

EQUIPMENT NEEDED:
a   *God Speaks to You: Volume 1*, Collins.
b   Photocopy from the Appendix (pp. 118-19) the time-chart of Old Testament history — one copy for each member of the group.
c   Photocopy from the Appendix (page 117) the 'Old Testament Library Quiz' – one copy for each member.
d   Prepare the 'Old Testament Bible Trail' as detailed below.
e   Notebooks; pens; Bibles.

Activity

Old Testament Library Quiz
Give each member of the group a copy of the time-chart, a Bible and a copy of the quiz. Ask them to complete the questions and then briefly discuss their answers.

Answers
i   2 Samuel: tenth century B.C.
ii   Psalms: eleventh century B.C.
iii Ezekiel: sixth century B.C.
iv   Deuteronomy: seventh century B.C.
v   Chronicles: fourth century B.C.
vi   Proverbs: tenth century B.C.

Old Testament Bible Trail
Now explain that they are going to go on an Old Testament journey. There are nine stages, each representing a different era of Old Testament history. The nine stages are:

Stage 1: Before Old Testament times
Stage 2: Abraham
Stage 3: Moses
Stage 4: Ten Commandments
Stage 5: The Ark
Stage 6: The Temple
Stage 7: Priests and Prophets
Stage 8: The Exile
Stage 9: After the Exile

THE OLD TESTAMENT

At each point in the trail (representing one of the nine stages), they will find a trail sheet with Bible references and questions on it. Explain that each member of the group will need a notebook, pencil and Bible. They are to follow the trail around the house and:

1 Write the stage number, date and headline in their notebook.
2 Look up the Bible references.
3 Write in their notebooks their answers to the questions on the trail sheet.

You could either go to each stage of the trail with the group and help them look up the Bible references, answer the questions and explain the significance of the events, or you could invite a parishioner to stand at each stage and explain what that stage is about. (This would need a good deal of preparation!) Another way of creating the trail would be to tape record a brief description of the events signified by each stage – using a variety of voices for the script – and then play the recording at each point.

You will need to prepare the trail in advance. The details for each stage are as follows:

Stage 1: Pre 1900 B.C. – Before Old Testament times
BIBLE REFERENCES: Deuteronomy 33:16
2 Samuel 5:23
Genesis 16:14
Genesis 28:18
Isaiah 34:14
QUESTION: Each of these references is to pre-Old Testament beliefs which the Jewish people may have inherited from their neighbours and earliest ancestors. What clues do you get from these verses about ancient beliefs? e.g. about sacred streams, stones, demons?

(*Information for leader:* the references refer, in order, to a belief in sacred trees; belief in sacred streams; belief in sacred stones; belief in demons.)

Stage 2: 1900-1700 B.C.: Abraham
BIBLE REFERENCES: Genesis 12:1-2
Genesis 13:14-15
QUESTION: What was the name of the man chosen by God to be founder of a great nation?

Stage 3: Approximately 1280? B.C.: Moses and the Exodus
BIBLE REFERENCE: Exodus 3:1-17
QUESTIONS: What was the name of God given to Moses?

What promise did God make to Moses and the people of Irael?

Stage 4: Approximately 1280? B.C.: The Ten Commandments
BIBLE REFERENCE: Exodus 20
QUESTION: How are these commandments normally described?

Stage 5: Approximately 1280-1200? B.C.: The Ark
BIBLE REFERENCE: Exodus 25:1-10
QUESTION: What was the purpose of the sanctuary?

Stage 6: c.959 B.C.: The Building of the Temple
BIBLE REFERENCES: 1 Kings 6:1-2
1 Kings 8:1-30
QUESTIONS: Who was the king of Israel when the Temple was built?
What was contained in the Ark of the Covenant?

Stage 7: c.700 B.C.: The Prophets
BIBLE REFERENCE: Amos 5:21-24
QUESTION: What did God require of the people, instead of fasts and sacrifices?

Stage 8: c.597 B.C.: The Exile
BIBLE REFERENCE: Jeremiah 39:1-10
QUESTIONS: Who was the king who took the people of Jerusalem to his own country?
What was that country called?

Stage 9: c.530 B.C.: The Return from Exile
BIBLE REFERENCE: Ezra 1:1-6
QUESTIONS: Who was the king who allowed the Jews to return to Jerusalem?
Of what country was he king?

★ ★ ★ ★ ★

By creating a time-trail like this, you should be helping the young people to get some idea of the pattern of Old Testament history.

At the end of the trail remind them of the journey they have made and explain that this was not just social and political history but also the history of increasing understanding of the nature of God – a history which led inevitably to the high expectation of the coming of the Messianic age.

II. THE LIFE OF THE CHURCH

6. The New Testament

AIM: To introduce the range of books in the New Testament.

EQUIPMENT NEEDED: Photocopies from Appendix (pp. 120-121); national and local newspapers; teenage/women's magazines; paper; pencils; and Bible.

Introduction
In the previous session combining an introduction to the Old Testament with a dash through two thousand years of history the young people were introduced to the Old Testament as a library of books. In this session the New Testament is the subject of the investigation.

Activity
Hand out to the group photo-copies of the two Letters from Children found in the Appendix (page 120). Discuss the letters and then invite each member of the group to write a letter to a famous personality expressing their views about a subject which matters deeply to them. Read the letters aloud and compare subjects.

Then look at the letters page of a national paper, a local paper and a teenage magazine and cut out the letters which really catch attention. Mount those letters on a sheet of paper and talk about why they seem important.

★ ★ ★ ★ ★

Invite the group to imagine that they have been imprisoned for their beliefs but that they are allowed to write one letter home every six months. What would they write? Compare their letters with the letter in the Appendix (page 120).

★ ★ ★ ★ ★

Following Jesus' death letters were written by the earliest disciples to the new Churches. Read Ephesians 1:1-2. Some of those early letters were written by Paul when he was in prison: read Philippians 1:12-14.

These letters were kept by the Churches which received them and were considered so important that they were eventually given the status of 'Scripture' and became part of the New Testament. It's worth pointing out that many of the Epistles were written before the Gospels.

Unlike the Old Testament there are only four varieties of book in the New Testament, viz: Gospels, History, Epistles and a strange dream-like book called 'Revelation'. Whereas the Old Testament represents almost two thousand years of history the New Testament represents at most one hundred years – and yet the books of the New Testament have had a colossal impact upon mankind.

And all this sprang from the life of one individual, Jesus of Nazareth.

The Gospels are accounts of his life, his teaching, his miracles and healings, and his eventual death and resurrection.

The History (the Acts of the Apostles) is the story of the first followers of Jesus after his death.

The Epistles are letters about his teaching and about his life in the Churches after his death and resurrection.

The Revelation of St John the Divine is a strange, visionary book which portrays Jesus and his followers caught up in a universal, cosmic drama of good and evil.

Together, all these books are the original and powerful documents of our faith. They need to be studied, explored, and read with care for they provide Christians with the nourishment needed in their journey towards God.

★ ★ ★ ★ ★

Just for fun: provide copies of the 'Jumbled Books Quiz' found in the Appendix (page 121) and ask the group to sort out the names.

Answers
Galatians; Revelation; Peter; Mark; Hebrews; John
Corinthians; Romans; Luke; Matthew; Acts; Philemon.

II. THE LIFE OF THE CHURCH

7. The Sacraments: Baptism

AIM: To explore the origins, meaning and significance of baptism.

EQUIPMENT NEEDED: Arrange to visit or meet at your local church.

Introduction
The Church has grown and changed through the centuries, but certain of its features have always been there. Amongst these are the two major sacraments, Baptism and Holy Communion. The word 'sacrament' has been defined in the Book of Common Prayer as 'an outward and visible sign of an inward and spiritual grace'. Perhaps the word 'focus' might also help in our understanding. Thus although God is always everywhere present he focusses grace and love in particular ways, and especially through the sacraments.

Before tackling the subject of baptism you will need to be clear what your parish policy is with regard to this sacrament. If possible try to arrange for the group to be present at a baptism service.

Activity
Visit your local church and make a special study of the font – is it old? New? Does it have any symbols carved on it? Where is it placed in relation to the rest of the church building? (In many old churches the font is near the main entrance to signify that baptism is the means of 'entering' the Church: in newer churches the font is often very close to the altar to show that it is at the heart of the Christian community.)

Look particularly for any symbols associated with the font e.g. an Alpha or an Omega to signify the beginning and the end, or perhaps a dove to symbolise the gift of the Holy Spirit. Discuss the meaning of the symbols with the group.

Then either use the poem 'The Font' by Clive Sansom (see below) or, for younger children, John Hencher's poem 'Water' (see below), and discuss the meaning of the poems concerning baptism

The Font
Thirty generations have stood and listened
By this flowering stone,
Wondering, pondering, as their child was christened;
Would he atone

For all disasters? – their son,
Now cleansed of sin,
Attain the ambitions they never won,
Would never win?

Child after child, generation on generation
Fails and fails.
Always, it seems, the subtle degradation
Of the world prevails.
Faith drowns: soon perish
The dreams they want;
Till they stand with the hopes their fathers cherish
Beside this font.

Some in stealth, raising the cover,
Have stolen water
To turn the thoughts of apprentice lover
Or merchant's daughter.
But in the end, servant or master,
In silk or cotton,
They have lain under marble and alabaster,
Or in graves forgotten . . .

Yet we see only the outward scheme.
Within the heart
There runs a parallel but opposing stream,
Ours yet apart,
Which flows from eternity and joins it there.
Who, on that level,
Can guess the final triumph or despair
Of God and Devil?

Who can divine through what
Red Seas they crossed,
Or on what ultimate rainbowed Ararat
Each Ark was tossed?
Stand here in faith who need
Such faith. Be reconciled.
Believe that your human love may lead
The inner child.

Water

When I was very young
An old man said to me,
Take care, all through your life,
Each and every day
Respect the power of WATER.

Washing my hands and face,
A long, hot bath in winter,
Turning on the taps,
Emptying the sink,
Releasing the flow of WATER.

Wet earth after the rain,
All the plants refreshed,
Trees drinking from their roots,
Enriching and reviving food,
Restored by the means of WATER.

Wide rivers and tiny streams
And ponds and reservoirs,
The locks, canals and springs,
Energy supplied by dams
Resisting the weight of WATER.

We need it for our thirst,
Approach its depth with care,
Tame it, save it, swim in it,
Embrace, enjoy and fear
Relentless might of WATER.

Wisdom of the Lord our God,
All praise to his name,
That we become his children,
Enter into his kingdom,
Reborn, baptised with WATER.

Invite the young people to tell a story based upon the font in your church. For example, suppose that the font is decorated with angels. Imagine a conversation between two angels after a baptism has taken place.

Or invite to the group a young family who have recently had a child baptised and get them to talk of their experience.

★ ★ ★ ★ ★

At baptism we believe that God gives the Holy Spirit to the person baptised; look up Mark 1:1-11 and remind the group of the origins of baptism from our Lord's own baptism. Then look up Matthew 28:18-20 and note how the early Church was commanded to baptise 'all peoples everywhere . . .' (*GNB*), and also look up Acts 2:37-41 – an account of the baptism of some of the first Christians.

* * * * *

Activity
Explain and explore the five symbols in baptism:
1 *Water* – indicating not only the washing away of sin but also a signal of the resurrection: i.e. the person baptised goes down into Christ's death and rises to new life.
2 *White clothes* – to show that the child has put on Jesus Christ like a garment and has been made new.
3 *Lighted candle* – a sign of the Easter faith.
4 *Signing with the cross* – a recognition both of the way membership of the Church has been given to us and of our fellowship with each other.
5 *Naming* – the giving of a Christian name also represents change from the old life to the new.

Any or all of these symbols could be explored by the group. For example, if you choose to concentrate on 'white clothes' you could investigate other occasions when special garments are worn e.g. weddings and funerals.

But whatever you do don't lose sight of the fact that you are trying to understand the layers of meaning and significance in the sacrament of Baptism.

II. THE LIFE OF THE CHURCH

8. The Sacraments
The Eucharist: Bread

AIM: To explore the origins, meaning and significance of the Eucharist.

EQUIPMENT NEEDED: A loaf of bread; colour magazines; scissors; paste; Prayer Book.

Introduction
From the very beginning of the Church's life the celebration of the Lord's Supper has been central. It is given a variety of names and each one of them lays emphasis on a different aspect. Thus: "Lord's Supper" emphasises the origin of the meal; it is a memorial. "Eucharist" meaning Thanksgiving, draws attention to the ever-present joy of the sacrament and the risen presence of Jesus; "Holy Communion" reminds us of its divine origin and its essentially communal nature; "Mass" has traditionally been associated with the concept of "sacrifice" but it also has a mission element – now the Mass is ended we are bidden to go out into the world to proclaim the faith.

Note
Clearly there are so many ways of tackling the centrality of the Eucharist that it's not possible to do justice to them all in one lesson. What we attempt here is to link together their own understanding of the symbolism of bread with biblical understanding, and that knowledge with the experience of the Eucharist in the life of the Church.

Activity
Place a loaf of bread on a plate. Cut a slice from the bread and hand pieces of it around the group. Explain that this is *not* a version of the Eucharist, but is a way of symbolising people's solidarity one with another. To share food, whether on a picnic or in a prison cell, is a way of expressing fellowship.

Read aloud the following:

>Be gentle when you touch bread
>Let it not lie uncared for, unwanted
>So often bread is taken for granted
>There is so much beauty in bread

> Beauty of rain and toil
> Beauty of sun and soil.
> The winds of the air caressed it
> Christ often blessed it
> Be gentle when you touch bread.
>
> *(Anon)*

The young people could copy this poem on to cards to keep with their prayer books or Bibles. (Do you have a calligrapher in your congregation who might like to help in the design of the cards?)

Look up the following references to Jesus taking bread in Mark's Gospel: Mark 8:1-9; 8:14-21. Compare Mark 8:6 with Mark 14:22; and then look at John 6:35. Discuss in what ways Jesus can be said to be 'The bread of life' today. After the discussion make a collage with a picture of a loaf of bread in the middle – and other pictures around it which give meaning to the Statement "I am the bread of life".

Then read Luke 24:13-32 paying particular attention to verse 30. Move from that into reading the Prayer of Consecration used in the Eucharist at your church, and link together in your commentary on it:
1. the poem: 'Be gentle when you touch bread'
2. the Feeding of the Multitude
3. John's meditation on Jesus 'The Bread of Life'
4. the collage on that theme

– and allow time in the group for them to discuss the layers of meaning and symbolism in the bread used at the Eucharist.

End the session by reading aloud the story of the Last Supper: Mark 14:12-25.

II. THE LIFE OF THE CHURCH

9. The Sacraments
The Eucharist: Wine

AIM: To explore the origins, meaning and significance of the Eucharist.

EQUIPMENT NEEDED: Bottle of wine; bunch of grapes; glass each; orange squash; colour magazines; scissors; paste.

Introduction
In the previous session we explored the symbolism of bread, and its use in the Eucharist. The other part of the Eucharistic sacrament is wine . . .

Activity
Place a bottle of wine in the centre of the group, and next to it a bunch of grapes. Give each member of the group a tumbler, and pour into each tumbler a quantity of orange squash or something similar. Ask them to imagine that they are at a wedding and that they are listening to a speech. At the end of the speech ask them to stand and drink a toast . . . .

Discuss with them the ways in which drinking is a highly symbolic activity. All the words associated with it: "Cheers", "Skol", "Good health . . ." etc. Then read aloud the following:

> Be loving when you drink wine
> So freely received and joyfully shared
> In the Spirit of him who cared
> Warm as a flowing river
> Shining and clear as the sun
> Deep as the soil
> of human toil
> The winds and the air caressed it
> Christ often blessed it.
> Be loving when you drink wine.
> *Giles Harcourt*

Again, the young people could copy this poem on to cards to keep with their prayer books or Bibles.

Look up the following references: Mark 2:22 – what was the new wine to which Jesus was referring? In what sense is Jesus' teaching still 'new wine' in our generation? Look at John's meditation/sermon on the theme of wine: John 2:1-10.

Read again the story of the Last Supper: Matthew 26:26-29 – and discuss the meaning of the actions: he took a cup
> gave thanks
> gave it to them

and the meaning of the words "Drink from it, all of you. For this is my blood, the blood of the new covenant, shed for many for the forgiveness of sins . . ."

Then compare the layers of symbolism in the three stories:
Jesus: the new wine, 'breaking the old mould' (Mark)
> the sharer of the new wine – shared with overflowing generosity (John)
> the wine as the promise of God to forgive and reconcile mankind . . .

Then try to portray these layers of meaning in a collage, much as you did with the symbolism of bread; i.e. a picture of a bottle of wine in the centre, and other pictures surrounding it to show various other meanings . . .

Move from that into reading the Prayer of Consecration used in your church and link together in your commentary on it:
1 the poem: 'Be loving when you drink wine'
2 the biblical references
3 the collage

End the session by reading Matthew's account of the Last Supper: Matthew 26: 14-35.

★ ★ ★ ★ ★

This session is a deliberate repetition in its style and activities of the previous lesson on 'bread' – the hope being that the one will reflect upon and deepen the other.

II. THE LIFE OF THE CHURCH

10. The Prayer Books

AIM: To introduce the Prayer Books used in the Church.

EQUIPMENT NEEDED: One copy of the *Book of Common Prayer* and one copy of *A.S.B. 1980* (*or the new services book) for each member; paper and pencils.

Introduction
The chances are that the young people in your group will have very little awareness of either the content or purposes of the Prayer Books used in the Church. The subject matter could appear a little dry but insofar as these Prayer Books deeply influence the lives of Anglican Christians, attention should be given to them.

Activity
Ask one member of the group to describe a place he or she knows well e.g. a small town, village or suburb. (It must not be a place known by others in the group.) As the speaker gives the description, invite each member of the group to make notes about the salient features. Allow this to go on for about five minutes. At the end of the five minutes give each young person a sheet of paper and ask them to draw a map of the place described. The speaker is also invited to draw a similar map. Allow five minutes or so for this. At that point compare the maps which have been drawn and, if possible, on one larger sheet of paper draw a map using features from the individual maps which sum up the area. (There's no need for meticulous drawing or scale measurements.)

The making of maps is a fascinating activity, and though we largely associate maps with geography they can be used for other areas of study as well. In a sense a Prayer Book is a kind of map. Firstly there comes the experience of God; then come attempts by individuals to 'map' that experience – in prayers, in worship etc.; then those individuals compare experiences and agree upon a common 'map'. Try looking at the Prayer Books like that. . . .

Provide each member with both a *Book of Common Prayer* and a copy of the A.S.B.* Turn to the Prefaces of each and read the opening sentence: in the *Book of Common Prayer* it says: "It hath been the wisdom of the Church of England ever since the first compiling of her Publick Liturgy, to keep the mean between two

---
*If you are not using this book in England, make the necessary adjustments to this lesson (e.g. in Australia, *An Australian Prayer Book*; in Ireland, *Alternative Prayer Book 1984*; in South Africa, *Liturgy '75*; in USA, *The Book of Common Prayer*.)

extremes, of too much stiffness in refusing, and of too much easiness in admitting any variation from it . . .". In the *A.S.B.* it says, with greater simplicity but, alas, much less beauty: "The Church of England has traditionally sought to maintain a balance between the old and the new". Both of those prefaces indicate very clearly the style and tone of the Prayer Books . . . but what do the Prayer Books contain?

Give a large sheet of paper to each group member and ask them to draw a line down the middle of the page, heading one side *Book of Common Prayer* and the other *A.S.B.* Explain that you are, as it were, going to create a 'map' of each book. The maps will not contain every single feature of each book, only the main features. Thus on the *Book of Common Prayer* side write Morning Prayer, Evening Prayer, Collects, Epistles and Gospels, Holy Communion, Baptism, Catechism, Confirmation, Marriage, Burial of the Dead, Psalter, the Ordination services. Do the same on the *A.S.B.* side – and down the middle of the paper create a series of symbols for each service e.g. baptism/water; marriage/ring etc.

Having drawn attention to the fact that there are two authorised Prayer Books in the Church, from this point on concentrate on whichever of those books is most used in your church.

1 Look up the collect for the week, read it aloud, and point out that there is a different collect for every week and every saint's day in the year, and that with that collect also goes an Epistle and Gospel reading. Get every member of the group to look up collects etc. for days in the Church year which you call out at random. (An obvious thing to do, but the intention is to help the young people to find their way around the book.)
2 Look up the Holy Communion Service, and find whichever version is used regularly at your church.
3 Look up Morning Prayer and Evening Prayer, and note that in the *Book of Common Prayer* it is explicitly stated: "daily to be said and used throughout the year". Is this the pattern in your church?
4 Look up the Psalter, and note that in the *A.S.B.* a psalm for each special day is appointed and can be found after the collect for that day.
5 Look up the Marriage service. When was that service last used in your church?

You could invite an elderly member of your congregation to come and say how they were taught to know the Prayer Book e.g. learning a collect by heart; and invite a younger member of the congregation to say what it is they like about the *A.S.B.* or the *Book of Common Prayer*.

Again, in one session it is impossible to cover all the ground, but the young people should, by the end, at least have the confidence to find their way around whichever Prayer Book your church uses.

II. THE LIFE OF THE CHURCH

11. The Church's timetable

AIM: To know the shape of the Church year.

EQUIPMENT NEEDED: Paper; lectionary.

Introduction
Young people are fully aware of the necessity for timetables. Their school lives are dictated by them on a daily, weekly and annual basis. The Church, like any institution, requires these kinds of timetables as well to help give it shape and purpose.

Activity
Invite the group to draw on a large sheet of paper their annual timetable, marking in holidays, week-ends, school terms, exams, Christmas etc. This should not be too detailed.

On another sheet of paper ask them to draw their weekly timetable during term-time, and again not too detailed.

Then ask each individual on a separate sheet of paper to map out their daily timetable e.g. get-up 7.15 a.m.; have breakfast, etc. . . .

Discuss the importance and necessity for timetables. Then alongside the group's annual timetable present the annual timetable of the Church – drawing attention to the major events of the Church's year e.g. Advent, Christmas, Lent, Easter, Ascension, Whitsun . . . and talk about the way this timetable is colour-coded e.g. Violet for Lent etc. Perhaps you could invite your sacristan to come to the lesson to explain how the 'colour-coding' works in practice. The colours are meant to represent the mood of each season of the Church's year, thus Violet for Lent indicates sorrow and penitence; White – joy; Green – 'new life'; Red – either fire or martyrdom.

Having established the shape of the Church's annual timetable, move on to look at the weekly timetable e.g. lesser saints' days; matins; evensong; holy communion, and perhaps you could add to this weekly parish events e.g. youth club; women's fellowships; Bible study groups. Draw the weekly timetable and compare it with their weekly timetable.

Then move from that to the daily timetable and explain that the Church has special Bible readings and psalms for each day of the year. Show the group the lectionary used in your church.

Invite your Vicar or Curate to come to this lesson to talk about 'their life': 'A Day in the life . . .' – and ask how their lives fit in with the timetable of the Church.

You could invite a member of your parish to create a slide-sequence of the annual life of the Church; or a slide-sequence of a week in the life. Obviously this would need preparation, but could be used on an annual basis not only for confirmation groups but perhaps as a means of showing newcomers how the parish ticks.

II. THE LIFE OF THE CHURCH

12. The Anglican Church now

AIM: To be aware of the diversity and extent of the Anglican Church.

EQUIPMENT NEEDED: An over-head projector, if possible, and prepared slides, plus a screen.

Introduction
The previous eleven sessions have been concentrated on 'The Life of the Church' and we have looked, even if briefly, at sacraments and Prayer Books and timetables amongst much else. Many, if not all of these things, are common to other churches – but the Anglican Church has a distinctive style and ethos which has much richness. The Anglican Church developed out of an extraordinarily turbulent period of history, but its origins lie well back before the Reformation. It claims and believes itself to be part of the 'Catholic' and 'Apostolic' Church i.e. it sees itself as 'Apostolic', founded on the teaching and authority of the apostles, fulfilling its calling by God to give itself to the world: it also sees itself as 'Catholic' i.e. part of the world-wide Church, the Church which extends through space and time. It believes that it has three strong strands in its life – scripture, tradition and reason, which need to be woven together in a balanced way.

Note
What is true of the Anglican Church is equally true of other churches, they have both a local, national and international dimension. If you are using this course in an ecumenical or a non-Anglican setting you will obviously have to alter the sessions accordingly.

Activity
Talk about those addresses you often see written by young people in their school rough-books i.e. Joe Bloggs, 15 Hope Street, Lower Snoddle, Longridge, Anyshire, England, UK, Europe, The World, The Universe . . . Those addresses are written as a kind of joke. If you wrote your address as a member of the Anglican Church you could write something very similar. Thus: Joe Bloggs, *Parish* of All Saints, *Deanery* of Longridge, *Diocese* of Barchester, *Province* of Canterbury, *Anglican* Communion.

Ask each member to write their Anglican 'address' on a sheet of paper and then explain what each part of the address means, thus:

THE LIFE OF THE CHURCH

Parish: Dating from the time the Church was established.
Deanery: An area containing several parishes.
Diocese: An area looked after by one or more bishops, having a Cathedral as its central Mother Church. A diocese is often the size of a county, or even larger. In England the boundaries are determined by Parliament, though many boundaries were fixed long before Parliament existed.
Province: A collection of dioceses under the leadership of an Archbishop. England, for example, is divided into two Provinces: Canterbury and York.
Anglican Communion: The Anglican Church has spread throughout the world and now has 27 provinces. The Archbishop of Canterbury is seen as the 'Chairman' of the Communion, and its focus of unity.

Each of those units, from the smallest, the parish, to the largest – the Anglican Communion – has a structure for decision making and designated leaders. Thus:

Parish: Looked after by the parish priest, the (Parochial) Church Council and Church Wardens.
Deanery: One of the clergy of the area is elected as Area or Rural Dean for a certain period of years. Each P.C.C. elects members to serve on the Deanery Synod – a Committee made up of both clergy and laymembers.
Diocese: The diocese is under the leadership and care of the Bishop, assisted by other bishops (suffragan bishops) and Archdeacons. Members of Deanery Synods are elected on to the Diocesan Synod.
Province: Under the leadership of the archbishop. In England the two provinces meet together twice a year for 'General Synod'.
Anglican Communion: There is an international body called the Anglican Consultative Council which meets regularly. The bishops and archbishops of the Anglican Church throughout the world meet every seven years at the Lambeth Conference.

* * * * *

Now: how can we present this in such a way that it can be understood? Probably the most effective method would be to use an Over-Head Projector with acetate slides, so that one can be laid on top of another to show the organisation of the Anglican Church – like circles in a pond.

You could ask your Diocesan Communications Officer to help with this. Could he or the Diocesan Education team make a display which could be used by all local parishes? You could suggest this to them.

★ ★ ★ ★ ★

Although it is right to emphasise the national and indeed the international scale of the Anglican Church, what the young people will be most familiar with is the Church in their parish. So, having introduced them to the wider scene focus your main attention on the Church locally.

You could invite a group of parishioners to give a three-minute talk (no more) to the group, for example: a Churchwarden; the Parish Council secretary; a Sunday School teacher; a caretaker; a Pastoral Assistant – asking them to explain very simply what they do in the parish and what motivates them.

Or: you could invite the Vicar/Curate to describe his work and compare the reality with the television caricatures and vice versa.

Or: you could ask a group of parishioners to prepare a slide sequence on the Church as they see it, or on the life of the parish.

Or: if the parish magazine is a good one, get a copy for each of the group and ask them to say what they think the Church looks like from reading it, and then, challenge the youngsters to produce a magazine of their own to explain what the Church and the parish seems like to them.

And finally
Discuss what the young people can get from the Church, but more importantly, what contribution they feel they can and should make to their Church and their community.

★ ★ ★ ★ ★

Note
Again, there's no way you can or should try to cover the range of the Church in one session. What you are aiming to do is to help the youngsters to have a sense of belonging to both a local and an international organisation – an organisation which is lively and growing.

★ ★ ★ ★ ★

These previous twelve sessions have tried to draw attention to some of the facets of the Life of the Church, beginning from the Pentecost experience and coming right up to date, via the Bible, Sacraments, Prayer Books and ecclesiastical organisation. It would be easy to become so detailed that you lose the sense of the sweep of history and the sense of a Church alive and growing in the present. That would be a pity. By bringing in lots of parishioners to the sessions this perspective of the living Church now can be maintained. In any case the next twelve sessions on 'The Life of a Christian' will help to keep it all in balance.

III. THE LIFE OF A CHRISTIAN

III. THE LIFE OF A CHRISTIAN

1. Prayer and worship

AIM: To appreciate the importance of personal commitment to prayer.

EQUIPMENT NEEDED: Balloons; felt-tip pens; string.

Introduction
There is little doubt that young people pray, though often in fragmentary fashion. They do not consider it necessary to pray regularly and steadily, but if they are to grow in their faith their prayer lives should be given attention and a bit of structure.

Activity
Give each young person a balloon. Ask them to blow it up and then to write on the balloon the most important truth they know; or, if they find that difficult, the gift they would most like to give to the world. When they have finished writing, discuss what they have said, and then ask them to tap the balloons into the air. Explain that prayer is very like that – it's tapping a balloon of hopes and problems up to God. Perhaps the exercise is a little banal but it gets across the essential simplicity and ease of prayer.

Move from that into rules for prayer. Look up Matthew 6:5-6, and discuss what Jesus teaches about prayer – the need for privacy and the need to be quiet. Are those conditions possible for the young people? Do they ever have any time when they feel they can be private and alone? Discuss this . . . Suggest places for prayer if they cannot find any space for peace and quiet at home e.g. on a school-bus; in church; walking to college . . . Take seriously the problem of finding privacy.

Then look at the question of how to pray. There's no need to go into great detail, but as well as exterior quietness, there is a need to quieten minds and bodies. This can be done by simply sitting still, or kneeling in a comfortable position for a brief period. Discuss with them why people seem to need to get their bodies organised before they pray and compare the merits and demerits of kneeling, sitting, standing and lying down.

Next comes the problem of how to give prayer a reasonable shape. You could suggest using the traditional pattern based on the word ACTS i.e. Adoration, Confession, Thanksgiving, Supplication; or the Five-Finger exercise based on the pattern of the hand i.e. the thumb being the strongest represents Adoration; the first finger points at others but in doing so three fingers point back at ourselves and this therefore represents Confession; the middle finger equals Thanksgiving; the fourth finger is Prayer for Others; and the little finger Prayer for Ourselves.

Hand each member of the group a length of string and ask them to tie a knot at the beginning to represent adoration; then another knot to represent confession etc.; but add a final knot to represent the prayer which sums up all prayer i.e. the Lord's Prayer.

So far then you have helped them to think about the surroundings for prayer, and the shape those prayers might have. No doubt the words 'Adoration', 'Confession', 'Supplication' etc. will need some exploration, and that is only right. But as far as possible aim at simplicity. You don't want to offer so many problems that you make prayer look like a highly technical and difficult exercise; but nor do you want to treat it so casually that they feel it has no importance. They need to see that prayer is simple – it is simply talking to God, knowing that God listens; but like all young people they do need to think about the structure of their prayers so that they are not idly repetitive. Perhaps they could consider either making a Diary of Prayer or using one which is ready-made e.g. *Be Thou My Vision* (Collins).

Young people are very active and need objects which can help them pray, which is why Brother Kenneth's idea of a string prayer is so helpful. There are other prayer-methods too, e.g. lighting a candle for someone, or holding a pebble in your hand as you pray and then carrying that pebble with you wherever you go.

Discuss all these possibilities with the group. Then end the session with a period of silence in which they can privately and silently decide on the form of prayer they themselves would like to use.

III. THE LIFE OF A CHRISTIAN

2. Rules for living: the Ten Commandments

AIM: To explore the necessity of rules for living.

EQUIPMENT NEEDED: Pen and paper.

Introduction
This session is based initially on playing games, and moves from that into a consideration of the relevance and importance of the Ten Commandments.

Activity

Game 1
Ask the young people to imagine that all the members of the group are the inhabitants of a 'pretend' country. Appoint one of the members as King/Queen. The members of the country are free to do what they like, but when the King/Queen makes a rule it has to be obeyed.

Let the game run for about ten minutes. At the end of that time each person must write down a list of the laws which have been decreed.

Compare that list of laws with the Ten Commandments: see Exodus 20: 1-17. Discuss which laws are similar and which are different. . . .

Game 2
Imagine a situation in which one of the rules of the pretend country has been broken. Appoint a Judge, counsel for the defence, counsel for the prosecution, a jury and witnesses. Invite one of the members to be the law-breaker, and then set the trial in motion. Allow the game to go on for as long as seems helpful – perhaps no more than ten or fifteen minutes. At the end ask the jury to consider their verdict and the Judge to pronounce sentence.

Discuss how the trial went, and how each participant saw the importance or otherwise of the procedure.

Then read Mark 2:23-28 and 3:1-6. Compare the events there with the events in the game. What were the similarities and differences?

Note
It would be quite wrong to belittle the law as understood at the time of Jesus. To the Jews the law, including the one concerning the Sabbath, had been given directly to Moses by God. That law was therefore divine and unalterable. But there was constant discussion about what actually constituted 'work' on the Sabbath . . . Jesus' answer to all this is utterly radical – 'The sabbath was made for man, not man for the sabbath'.

Return to Exodus 20:1-17 and read the Ten Commandments aloud. Ask each member to write the Ten Commandments down in a notebook. If there is time discuss the significance of these commandments for life in the twentieth century.

III. THE LIFE OF A CHRISTIAN

3. Rules for living: the Summary of The Law

AIM: To consider how to keep Jesus' summary of the law.

EQUIPMENT NEEDED: Newspaper cuttings and photographs.

Introduction
On the whole, the previous session will have concentrated on the negative side of the law: 'Thou shalt not'... Jesus' summary of the law emphasised the positive: 'Thou shalt'.

Activity
Give each member of the group a newspaper cutting of a major news story – minus the headline. Ask them to read the story carefully and then invent a suitable headline. Compare the headlines they create with those created by the original sub-editors.

Remind the class of the previous lesson and then read aloud Mark 12:28-34. Each person should write down that summary of the law in their notebooks.

What Jesus had been asked for by the lawyers was a kind of headline – a memorable summary of all the complex laws. The summary Jesus gave has become the basis ever since of Christian morality and therefore needs to be considered very carefully.

★ ★ ★ ★ ★

Cut out from magazines and newspapers a variety of photographs of non-famous people. Give a photograph to each youngster and ask them to study the photograph carefully. Get each of them to write a brief character-description of their photograph/personality, and discuss those descriptions in the group. Ask each person then to imagine that some tragedy, disaster or misfortune has happened to their photograph/personality – how would they or should they react? What does Jesus mean when he gives the command: 'Love your neighbour as yourself'? What are the problems to be overcome in keeping that order?

★ ★ ★ ★ ★

Having discussed a variety of hypothetical situations invite the group to think very carefully about the parish in which they live. When Jesus says 'Love your neighbour as yourself', what could and should that mean in practice? Are there any community needs which the young people ought to meet? Again, be very practical and down-to-earth; and work out if their analysis of the local situation is accurate and, if it is, what they can actually do to help either as a group or individually.

You could invite to the group people from the community who are already involved in the 'caring' professions e.g. a probation officer or nurse; or, indeed, a representative from one of the Church's organisations e.g. Church of England Children's Society, to tell the young people of their work.

★ ★ ★ ★ ★

In the previous session and in this one the emphasis has been on rules for Christian living. There is a tradition in the Church which encourages every Christian to have a 'Rule of Life'. Perhaps there are members of, say, the Franciscan 'Third Order' in your parish or area, who could be invited in to speak about the 'rule of life' they keep. Discuss the 'Rule of Life' idea and ask each individual to devise a rule of life for themselves in which the 'Summary of the Law' is given practical expression.

III. THE LIFE OF A CHRISTIAN

4. Forgiveness

AIM: To explore the importance of forgiveness for Christians.

EQUIPMENT NEEDED: Paper; Prayer Books.

Introduction
It is tempting to keep Christianity safe and manageable by turning it into yet another set of religious rules. Important as rules are, there is at the heart of the New Testament a radically disturbing element which will not be tied down. This is the element of forgiveness.

Activity
Set the scene: choose one person as 'Mother', another as 'Father', and a third as the teenager. The situation is this. The parents have allowed the teenager to stay out until 11 p.m. It is now 11.45 p.m. and he creeps through the front door. A conversation follows. . . .

Allow the role play to develop as it will. When you feel the time is ripe draw it to a close and lead the discussion towards the notion of 'Forgiveness'. Is 'Forgiveness' part of this stereo-typed family situation? If it seems not to be, discuss with the group a situation which could be more relevant e.g. marital disharmony; stealing from a brother or sister . . . and explore that situation in a role play.

At the end of these role plays consider Jesus' teaching about forgiveness. Look up Matthew 6:14-15 – where forgiveness is seen to be related to God's relationship with us. "If you do not forgive others then the wrongs you have done will not be forgiven by your Father."

Discuss those situations where it is very, very difficult to forgive. Why are they so difficult? What can be done about it?

Look up Matthew 5:38-42, read the passage aloud and encourage discussion about it. Do they feel that the demands are impossible or do they think that if they were kept life could be transformed? Are there situations they themselves are in which require this kind of treatment?

Allow time for discussion of this important subject, and then consider the way the Church also provides the context to pray for forgiveness i.e. in worship at the time of General Confession. At this point someone may well ask about 'Private' confession. In the Anglican Church the saying is "All may; none must; some should." A priest is empowered to hear confessions, to keep the 'seal of the confessional' i.e. the confession is completely and utterly confidential; and to pronounce absolution. In some parts of the Church private confession is regularly practised, in others hardly at all. But it should be widely known to be available to any who require it.

Look at the confession in the Prayer Book you use in your church and discuss what it means. But also look at the words of absolution: the assurance of God's forgiveness is proclaimed. Discuss this too.

Get the group to draw a symbol for both 'confession' and 'absolution'.

Note that the confession expresses the solidarity of all mankind in sin. Sin is not just an individual matter, it can seem to infect systems as well. Discuss this problem in the group relating it to specific situations e.g. apartheid; north/south divide; haves/have-nots etc.

At the end of the session you could all say together the words of the General Confession and the words of the absolution altering the words from 'you' to 'us' if necessary, using the group symbols as the focus for your attention.

III. THE LIFE OF A CHRISTIAN

5. The new way

AIM: To see the radical nature of following Jesus.

EQUIPMENT NEEDED: Candle; bowl of salt; Bibles.

Introduction
Following Jesus requires a daily and continuous transformation of our values and attitudes. Young people are at the beginning of their journey on 'the way' and it is wrong to load them up with all kinds of heavy and unnecessary baggage. But they need to be aware that their journey will involve serious decision-making and can be costly.

Activity
Darken the room, so that the group sits in complete darkness (they are bound to giggle – so wait for that to subside). Then light a candle and read aloud Matthew 5:14:

> "You are light for all the world. A town that stands on a hill cannot be hidden. When a lamp is lit, it is not put under the meal-tub but on the lamp-stand, where it gives light to everyone in the house. And you, like the lamp, must shed light among your fellows so that, when they see the good you do, they may give praise to your Father in heaven."

You might again wait in silence after the reading and ask them to think about its meaning, or after a suitable pause read the passage again. Then with the candle still lit discuss what they believe Jesus meant when he described his disciples as 'light for all the world'. What does it mean for the young people now?

When the discussion is concluded pass around a small bowl containing salt. Invite everyone present to take a pinch and put it on their tongue and then read: Matthew 5:13:

> "You are salt to the world. And if salt becomes tasteless, how is its saltiness to be restored?"

Jesus seems to be describing how his followers should be, in two contradictory ways – very obvious and 'up-front' as a light; hidden and yet important like salt. What do light and salt have in common? In what ways are they different? In what ways can young Christians be like 'salt'? Note that the injunction to be like light and like salt comes after the 'Sermon on the Mount'. Read Matthew 5:1-10 aloud.

Then split the class up into threes giving each trio one of the Beatitudes to discuss. At the end of five minutes each trio has to report back to the main group what they believe their particular Beatitude means. If they would like to illustrate their findings with a drawing so much the better.

Ask each member to copy out the Beatitudes into their notebooks and, if possible, to learn them by heart (why not?).

The Beatitudes lend themselves to choral speaking. If you have someone in your parish who could teach the group to present the Beatitudes at worship in choral speech that would be good.

At the end of the session darken the room again, light the candle, and simply read the whole of Matthew 5:1-16 to sum up the session.

III. THE LIFE OF A CHRISTIAN

6. The great divide?

AIM: To consider the ethical consequences of following Jesus.

EQUIPMENT NEEDED: *The Last Battle* by C.S. Lewis; video or tape/slide equipment.

Introduction

To follow Jesus is not just about an individual's relationship with God, it also has consequences for his relationships with his fellow people. It is no longer fashionable to think much about the 'Last Judgement', though there was a time when pictures and sculptures of the Last Judgement were common in many churches. The fact that fashion has changed should not blind us to the reality that much of Jesus' message was about God's justice as well as God's love. The subject is difficult to tackle and should be handled with much sensitivity.

Activity

either

If there is a church or cathedral nearby (or art gallery) which has a painting or sculpture of the Last Judgement, go to see it and discuss with the young people why they think the artist chose that as his subject. Why is it no longer fashionable as a subject? (You'll probably need the help of an art teacher with this.) Quite often these scenes are above the entrance to churches – why might that be?

or

If such a visit is not possible and if you don't have an art teacher who would be willing or able to come to the group to talk about the nature and history of Christian art, then you will have to tackle this topic differently. Thus, read aloud an extract from *The Last Battle* by C.S. Lewis. The extract to use is from chapter 14, beginning 'The light from behind them (and a little to their right) was so strong . . . and Farsight the Eagle, and the dear Dogs and the Horses, and Poggin the Dwarf.' (Pages 144-147 of the Fontana edition.) Discuss what the story reveals about choice and judgement. Follow it with Matthew 25: 31-46. If that is how God judges our behaviour what consequences flow from it? Who are the poor, the hungry, the imprisoned etc. for whom we ought to care?

Then, either show a video/tape-slide sequence of the work of one of the Christian agencies e.g. Christian Aid; Tear Fund; CAFOD; or invite a speaker from one of those agencies to talk to the group about their ministry.

Look at the way your own parish works. In what ways are Jesus' injunctions to care for the poor, hungry etc. actually practised – and in what ways can the young people take part?

III. THE LIFE OF A CHRISTIAN

7. Telling the truth

AIM: To consider the importance of Christian truthfulness.

EQUIPMENT NEEDED: Tape-recorder.

Introduction
If you conducted a poll amongst your youngsters to discover which categories of people they believe can be relied on to tell the truth it might be surprising. (Perhaps you could try it.) As followers of Christ, truthfulness and trustworthiness should be amongst their strongest characteristics. But, what is truth . . .?

Activity
a Read aloud John 18:33-38, with one person being the narrator, another Pilate, and another Jesus. At the end of the reading ask Pilate to imagine that he is being interviewed by a radio station interested in his decision. Appoint one member to be the interviewer and tape-record the interview. When the interview is finished listen to the tape together and discuss it.

b Read aloud John 9:1-38 with one person as narrator and others as
   (i)   the disciples   (iv) neighbours
   (ii) the blind man   (v) Pharisees
   (iii) Jesus   (vi) parents of the blind man
   Appoint one member to interview each group/character in turn, trying to establish the truth of the situation as they saw it. When the interview is finished listen to the tape together and discuss it.

c Set up a role play involving a school-teacher, pupils and a shop-keeper. The scene is this: the shop-keeper is convinced that one of the pupils has been shop-lifting. He comes to school to see the teacher. . . . Take the scene on from there. At the end of the role play ask the 'radio-interviewer' to conduct an enquiry to try to discover what really happened. Listen to the tape and discuss it.

In all three activities the topic under discussion is 'Truth'. When Jesus said "My task is to bear witness to the truth" – what did he mean? Equally when he says "I am the way, I am the truth and I am the life", to what kind of truth is he referring?

If Jesus' task is to bear witness to the Truth, what kind of expectations should there be of his followers? Discuss with the group the situations in which they find telling the truth very difficult.

★ ★ ★ ★ ★

Is there an adult in the congregation e.g. solicitor, doctor, teacher, nurse, mechanic, whose professional life is much concerned with truth, who could share in this session and bring their experience to bear?

★ ★ ★ ★ ★

The group could create a design for a stained-glass window on the theme "I am the truth".

III. THE LIFE OF A CHRISTIAN

8. Sharing gifts

AIM: To appreciate their own gifts and the need to share them.

EQUIPMENT NEEDED: Pencils, black paper, scissors; Bible; Prayer Book.

Activity
Split the group into pairs and ask each pair to draw a silhouette of each other. Transfer those silhouettes on to black paper. Stick a single silhouette on to one large sheet of paper. Provide everyone with a felt-tip pen and ask the group to write on each sheet of paper the gifts they believe the silhouetted person has. Obviously the person whose silhouette it is is not allowed to describe his or her own gifts.

At the end of this discuss with them the surprises, the omissions and the range of gifts in the group, e.g. of music, drawing, athletics, humour, wit etc.

Then read Matthew 25:14-30 – a parable about God's Kingdom. In what ways can that parable be understood for our times? (You could dramatise this Gospel passage and present it in church.)

Look at the Prayer Book used at your Eucharist. In some churches these words are spoken at the Peace: "We are the Body of Christ. In the one Spirit we were all baptised into one body. Let us then pursue all that makes for peace and builds up our common life." Bearing those words in mind ask the group to think of ten members of the congregation whom they know and list their gifts. Make a complete list, omitting names, of the gifts of your church and present it either for display or to be taken up as part of the Offertory procession on a Sunday.

Recall or read the story of the Wise Men and the gifts they brought to the Infant Christ – which gifts does each individual feel he or she would most want to offer Christ as a thank-offering? Discuss the choice.

Having listed the known and obvious gifts of the group, ask if they would be willing to discuss the gifts they would like to have. (This requires much sensitivity, so don't handle it if you feel doubtful). Then discuss how those gifts may be hidden or how, if they are realistic, they could be developed.

At the end of the session ask them to picture in their minds one of the silhouettes and to pray in silence for that person, giving thanks for their gifts.

III. THE LIFE OF A CHRISTIAN

9. Death and life eternal

AIM: To explore the implications of the Resurrection.

EQUIPMENT NEEDED: Copies of the texts in the Appendix (pp. 121-4).

Introduction
A belief in life beyond death is found in every culture in every continent. It is not a belief confined to Christianity alone, but in Christ Jesus we believe that the hint and promise of life eternal has become reality.

Activity
There are several ways of tackling this topic: which one you choose will depend upon your particular circumstances and the youngsters themselves. You could:
a   Take them either to the church or the churchyard and ask them to write down all those quotations they see on the memorial tablets and the tombstones. Then return to the meeting room to discuss what they have discovered. How many of the quotations refer to eternal life?
b   Invite a nurse or doctor or chaplain from a hospice nearby to talk to the group about their work and the beliefs that sustain them and the patients.
c   Circulate the passages in the Appendix (pp. 121-4) and discuss what the young people think they mean. Ask them which of those readings they find most helpful.
d   Ask each individual to design an Easter card, compare it with the others and after discussion get the group to design a card taking into account all that they have learnt from each others designs.

Then read aloud John 20:1-23 and discuss the resurrection appearance of Jesus. Look at the Eucharistic Prayer used in your church and ask the group to read it silently and to note how central the resurrection of Jesus is to that prayer. Then read aloud this post-Communion prayer and note again how the prayer is shot through with the hope of life through death . . .

> Father of all, we give you thanks and praise, that when we were still far off you met us in your Son and brought us home. Dying and living, he declared your love, gave us grace, and opened the gate of glory. May we who share Christ's body live his risen life; we who drink his cup bring life to others; we whom the Spirit lights give light to the world. Keep us firm in the hope you have set before us, so we and all your children shall be free, and the whole earth live to praise your name; through Christ our Lord. Amen.
>
> *(A.S.B. 1980)*

Try then to combine the experience and hopes of the Church as expressed in its buildings and liturgy; the resurrection of Jesus as written in the Gospels, with the natural hopes, fears and problems of the young people themselves. You will need to encourage the discussion to be sensitive and careful and undogmatic and to be very aware of any who might find it all too much e.g. if they themselves have recently been bereaved. If this latter is the case be especially careful.

You may also find, especially amongst older teenagers, a sense of despair. It's often expressed by 'What's the point? I get up, go to school, come home, do my homework, go to bed, get up. . . .' They see themselves as caught on a kind of wheel off which they cannot get – and at the same time they have become acutely aware of some of the absurdity and pain of the world. It all seems so hopeless. If this kind of area is explored it needs to be done with sensitivity. The despair should be listened to seriously. For a Christian, Jesus' resurrection is not only a sign of hope at death, but it also brings new life to those situations which have some of the characteristics of death, and especially in moments of utter despair. "My God. My God. Why have you forsaken me?" is a cry all human beings, including teenagers, can utter.

Round off the session by saying the prayer given above.

III. THE LIFE OF A CHRISTIAN

10. "I believe"

AIM: To explore the relationship between Creeds and personal belief.

EQUIPMENT NEEDED: Tape-measure; foot gauge; plumb-line; spirit level; (optional) exercise bike with speedometer; scales; Prayer Book.

Introduction
Young people so often believe that if they are a Christian they have to swallow all the doctrines hook, line and sinker. It's a false impression. There is a fine balance to be kept by all Christians between doubt, faith and belief. Gullibility is not a Christian virtue; to search openly for the truth is.

Activity
Begin the session relatively quietly i.e. ask each person to stand up against a wall and have their height measured. Make a chart with the recorded height. Then carry out the same procedure by weighing everyone; and, if you can borrow a foot-gauge from a shoe-shop, measure everyone's feet. Simply draw attention to the fact that as human beings we are physically measurable.

Go on from that to show them how a plumb-line works, and how a spirit level acts as an accurate gauge.

Then, if you can borrow it and for the sheer fun of it, let each member ride on an exercise bike and see how fast they can go . . ..

At the end of all these activities discuss the importance of measurement, but also note that all measurements are relative. Firstly, for example, in measuring height you can use the metric system or the Imperial 'feet and inches' scale; in speed you can measure either m.p.h. or k.p.h. Discuss the function and purpose of measurement i.e. to set a reasonable standard.

Then ask each person to write down on a sheet of paper a definition of beauty and a means of measuring it. Discuss their findings with them. Move on from that to look at the Creeds. The Creeds are, as it were, scales of measurement constructed at particular periods in the history of the Church (and are therefore affected by the way people thought in those days). They remain as useful measures of orthodoxy. Look at this early formula of the Creed (used in the *A.S.B. 1980* Baptism and Confirmation services):

Do you believe and trust in God the Father,
who made the world?
I believe and trust in him.

Do you believe and trust in his Holy Spirit,
who gives life to the people of God?
I believe and trust in him.

Do you believe and trust in his Son Jesus Christ,
who redeemed mankind?
I believe and trust in him.

This is the faith of the Church.
This is our faith.
We believe and trust in one God,
Father, Son, and Holy Spirit.
(A.S.B. 1980)

and compare it with one of the other Creeds e.g. the Apostle's Creed or even the Athanasian Creed found in the *Book of Common Prayer*. Discuss the differences between them.

Ask each member to attempt to write their own creed i.e. 'I John Smith believe . . .' This will be a difficult exercise. Compare their versions with each other and with the creeds as given in the Prayer Books, and with the expression of belief made at their baptism. What are the similarities and what are the differences? Could they write a group creed? Encourage them not only to treat the orthodox Creeds very seriously but also to go on thinking carefully about their own beliefs.

Discuss whether or not they feel able to take part in the statement of belief in the Confirmation service, but remind them that what we believe and how we believe changes as we grow up and develop. Some beliefs are quite properly only provisional, as indeed are some doubts, but both belief and doubt are part and parcel of a Christian's life.

III. THE LIFE OF A CHRISTIAN

11. I belong

AIM: To appreciate and understand belonging to Jesus and the Church.

EQUIPMENT NEEDED: Paper; felt-tip pens.

Introduction
All of us need a sense of belonging – to a family, a community, a country. It's that same sense of belonging which draws people to Christ and the Church. St Augustine put it succinctly: "Our hearts are restless till they find their rest in Thee." Young people have a strong sense of that restlessness and often wonder where on earth they belong.

Activity
Split the group into two teams and play a game of charades. Follow that with the same teams playing a game of 'Shop'. The game is simple. One team decides on the kind of shop it will represent e.g. Ironmongers, and each member of that team is given one word to describe an item in that shop, thus: nut; bolt; knife; fork etc. The opposing team then ask the shop team to say either 'loudly' or 'softly' what the objects are – and the shop team shouts or whispers the names all together. The opposition have to guess what kind of shop is represented.

After the games discuss what it meant to belong to the team; and lead the discussion on to discuss all the other groups and teams to which individuals belong e.g. family; cadets; scouts, guides; rugby; hockey etc. Move on from that to discuss what it means to belong to the Church – what are the obligations? the benefits? the duties? the rights?

Either
Invite as many adults from the Church as there are young people in the group. Pair off each adult with each youngster and invite them to talk together for five minutes. At the end of the five minutes the adult has to introduce the young person to the group and the young person the adult. It might be easier, to save adolescent embarrassment, for the introductions to be done in a different way. The couple could be given a sheet of paper and on that paper have to draw two symbols, one for the adult and one for the youngster. The symbols should contain indications of interests, work, hobbies etc. When completed the adult could introduce the symbols to the rest of the group. The idea is to try to establish a sense of belonging between adult and young person in the Church.

Or
Visit your church and look out especially for any signs which show what it means to belong – banners, badges, logos, posters. Invite each individual to design a poster to show what it means to belong to that church. Discuss the posters together and then design a group poster using ideas culled from the individual ones.

★ ★ ★ ★ ★

Whilst we all undoubtedly belong to the Church the root cause of that belonging is Jesus Christ. He it is to whom we primarily belong. Read aloud the call of the disciples:
  Mark 1:14-20
  Mark 2:13-14
  Mark 3:13-19
Discuss what the call to follow Jesus meant for those first disciples, and what that call means for young people today.

Read to the group the passage 'Rule for a new brother' which is about seeking God, from the Appendix (pp. 124-5), and end the session either with that or with the St Richard of Chichester prayer: "O most merciful redeemer, friend and brother, may I know thee more clearly, love thee more dearly and follow thee more nearly, day by day. . . ."

III. THE LIFE OF A CHRISTIAN

12. Into the future . . .

AIM: To think about the future and Jesus' presence within it.

EQUIPMENT NEEDED: Extract from a science fiction book (or video); Tape-recorder; prepared book-mark; Bible; chalice; candle.

Introduction
The famous opening words of 'Star Trek' will probably be known to you: ". . . to boldly go where no man has gone before . . ." etc. Whether or not any of the more bizarre science fictions will become science fact in the lifetime of the young people is a matter for debate but they will face a rapidly changing world as they grow up. How will they cope? What difference will their Christian faith make to them?

Activity
Read a passage from any science-fiction book you know, or show a clip from a video of, for example, 'Star Trek' or '2010'. Then ask the individuals to imagine themselves in twenty years time – what would they like to be doing? Where will they be living? You could record this as a radio-interview with a tape-recorder if you wished. Encourage them to day-dream. Or perhaps they would prefer to draw the future. Get them to design a futuristic house or a futuristic town and discuss it with them. Will there be any need in that town for a church?

Prospects for the future have always intrigued mankind – look up Revelation 21:1-7; and discuss how far that is still people's dream for the ideal future – no pain, no wars, no sorrow . . ..

Then discuss how relevant and important they believe their faith will be to them as they grow up.

Read Matthew 28:16-20 – the promise that the risen and ascended Christ will be with his followers until the end of time. How far does the group believe that and accept it? What are their doubts? What are their certainties?

Discuss the qualities they feel they will need to face the future, and compare what they say with St Paul's list in Ephesians 6:10-18.

Then put in the centre of the group: a *Bible*; a *chalice* and a *candle*:

The *Bible* represents God the Father who will sustain them wherever they go.

The *Chalice* represents God the Son who will pour his love into their hearts and lives.

The *Candle* represents God the Holy Spirit who will be their light in the years ahead.

Then say this prayer to end the session: it was written by Dag Hammerskjold, a former Secretary-General of the United Nations:

> "Lord, for what has been: thanks
> to what shall be: Yes."

– and give a copy of that prayer, on a book-mark, to every member of the group.

Appendix

SESSION II:5 – THE OLD TESTAMENT

1 The Old Testament Library Quiz
In boxes below (arranged like books in a library), write the name of one of the Old Testament Bible books which:
i   Represents history.
ii Represents songs.
iii Represents prophecy.
iv Represents Laws.
v   Represents history.
vi Represents Proverbs.

| C | P | 2S | P | E | D |

THE OLD TESTAMENT

Check these names against the Time-Chart and see if you can find which century they were written in. Write the date of the century on the base of the 'books' on the 'bookshelf' above.

APPENDIX

2 The Old Testament Time-Chart

The dates given below may be a help to you in getting a grasp of Old Testament history. Many of the dates are approximate:

B.C.			
1900-1700	The Patriarchs (Abraham, Isaac, etc.) in Palestine		
1700-1300	The Hebrews in Egypt		
1280?	The Exodus: Hebrews led by Moses leave Egypt		
1250-1200	The Hebrews conquer Palestine (The 'Promised Land') (Beginning of Iron Age: 1200-1000)		
1200-1020	The Period of the Judges (Philistines settle in Palestine)		
			Literature
1020-	Saul becomes king		Early poems and stories
1004-	David becomes king		Early psalms
966-	Solomon becomes king		Early proverbs
922	'Israel' splits into two kingdoms: (1) The kingdom of Judah (922-587) (2) The kingdom of Israel (922-721)		
	Israel	*Judah*	
926-901	Jeroboam 1	Rehoboam 926-910	2 Samuel 9-20
850	Ahab (871-852)	Jehosaphat 872-852	Part of Pentateuch
Eighth Century	721: Israel invaded by Assyrians	701: Judah invaded by Assyrians	Elijah and Elishah stories Amos Hosea Parts of Isaiah Micah
Seventh Century			Deuteronomy
Sixth Century		597-586: Departed to Babylon 586: end of independence 538: Babylon conquered by Persians Jews return to Palestine 520-516: Temple at Jerusalem rebuilt	Nahum Zephaniah Habbakuk Jeremiah Ezekiel Lamentations Isaiah 40-55 Obadiah Haggai Zechariah 1-8

APPENDIX

Fifth Century		Malachi Isaiah 56-66 Ruth Jonah Job? Joel? Nehemiah
Fourth Century	336-323: Alexander the Great conquers the Persian Empire	Ezra Pentateuch in final form Chronicles
Third Century	Palestine a province of Egypt (ruled by Ptolemy – one of Alexander the Great's Generals – until c.200). The ruled by the Seleucids until . . .	Song of Songs Ecclesiastes
Second Century	. . . Maccabean revolt: 168-167	Ecclesiasticus Zechariah 9-14 Tobit Daniel Esther
A.D. First Century	Some time at the end of the first century A.D. the 'canon' of the Old Testament was fixed.	
Tenth Century	The oldest complete manuscript of the Old Testament we have comes from the 10th Century	

APPENDIX

SESSION II:6 – THE NEW TESTAMENT

1 Letters from Children

Dear Teacher,

When you are asked a question, I don't like the way you answer it. You often reply saying, 'Well I am not sure', or 'I'll see', or 'perhaps'. I feel that you just can't be bothered to think of a proper answer and so you dismiss the question by saying one of the above.

Another thing that I don't like about you is that you don't like being told that you are wrong by a child. I find this very irritating and you seem to think that you are far too superior to make a mistake.

I think that you are not too bad at teaching but when we do homework we have to wait ages for it to be marked and I don't like that. If we have made the effort to do it, you should make the effort to mark it as soon as possible.

Andrew (14 years)

Dear Mr President,

I have often stayed awake at night wondering if it is true that the end of the world is at a touch of a button. What I mean is, is it true that the world could be blown up by one bomb? This thought frightens me tremendously, but I am equally frightened of the thought of a nuclear world war. I understand that you must also think about this and do not know the answer. But I would be interested in your opinion and thoughts over the two matters.

Thank you,

Elizabeth (14 years)

2 An extract from a letter by a Christian imprisoned for her faith

How good it is that the small craft of my life is being steered by the hand of the good Father. When he is at the helm nothing is to be feared. Then, no matter how difficult life may be, you will know how to resist and love. I can say that the year 1975 has flown by like a flash, it has been a year of joy for me. I thank the good Lord for it . . .

We have many old women and sick people, so I rejoice that I have been brought here in accordance with my calling – to nurse and to love. Although I long greatly to see you all, it will be hard for me to leave here. It will be distressing to leave people who have become so near and dear to me, but the good Lord does indeed care for us most of all . . .

APPENDIX

3   New Testament 'Jumbled Books' Quiz

TALGAINSA   THINNROCIAS
EVELNATIOR   NORAMS
TREPE   KLUE
KRAM   TWETHAM
SWEBREH   STAC
NOHJ   MLHNPOEI

SESSION III:9 – DEATH AND LIFE ETERNAL

1   On dying

Death is nothing at all – I have slipped away into the next room – I am I, and you are you – whatever we were to each other, that we are still. Call me by my own familiar name, speak to me in the easy way which you always used. Put no difference into your tone; wear no forced air of solemnity or sorrow. Laugh as we always laughed at the little jokes we enjoyed together. Play, smile, think of me, pray for me. Let my name be ever that household word that it always was. Let it be spoken without effort, without the ghost of a shadow on it. Life means all that it ever meant. It is the same as it ever was. There is absolutely unbroken continuity.

What is death but a negligible accident?

Why should I be out of your mind because I am out of your sight?

I am waiting for you for an interval somewhere very near, just round the corner.

All is well.

Henry Scott Holland

2   A prayer for the departed

We seem to give them back to you, O God, who gave them to us . . . Yet as you did not lose them in giving, so we do not lose them by their return. O lover of souls, you do not give as the world gives. What you give you do not take away; for what is yours is ours also if we are yours. And life is eternal and love is immortal; and death is only a horizon; and a horizon is nothing save the limit of our sight. Lift us up, strong son of God, that we may see further; cleanse our eyes that we

APPENDIX

may see more clearly; draw us closer to yourself that we may know ourselves to be nearer to our loved ones who are with you. And while you prepare a place for them, prepare us also for that happy place, that where you are we may be also for evermore. Amen.

Bishop Charles Henry Brent 1862-1929 (adapted)

3   An extract from *The Pilgrim's Progress* by John Bunyan

(Christian and Hopeful have come through the river of death.)

Now upon the bank of the river, on the other side, they saw the two shining men again, who there waited for them. Wherefore being come out of the river, they saluted them, saying, We are ministering spirits, sent forth to minister for those that shall be heirs of salvation. Thus they went along towards the fate.

Now you must note, that the City stood upon a mighty hill; but the pilgrims went up that hill with ease, because they had these two men to lead them up by the arms; also they had left their mortal garments behind them in the river; for though they went in with them, they came out without them. They therefore went up here with much agility and speed, though the foundation upon which the City was framed was higher than the clouds; they therefore went up through the regions of the air, sweetly talking as they went, being comforted because they had safely got over the river, and had such glorious companions to attend them.

The talk that they had with the shining ones was about the glory of the place; who told them that the beauty and glory of it was inexpressible. There, said they, is the Mount Sion, the heavenly Jerusalem, the innumerable company of angels, and the spirits of just men made perfect. You are going now, said they, to the paradise of God, wherein you shall see the tree of life, and eat of the never-fading fruits thereof: and when you come there you shall have white robes given you, and your walk and talk shall be every day with the King, even all the days of eternity. There you shall not see again such things as you saw when you were in the lower region upon the earth: to wit, sorrow, sickness, affliction and death; for the former things are passed away. The men then asked, What must we do in the holy place? To whom it was answered, You must there receive the comfort of all your toil, and have joy for all your sorrow; you must reap what you have sown, even the fruit of all your prayers, and tears, and sufferings for the King by the way. In that place you must wear crowns of gold, and enjoy the perpetual sight and visions of the Holy One; for there you shall see him as he is. There also you shall serve him continually.

APPENDIX

4   An extract from *Watership Down* by Richard Adams

One chilly, blustery morning in March, I cannot tell exactly how many springs later, Hazel was dozing and waking in his burrow. He had spent a good deal of time there lately, for he felt the cold and could not seem to smell or run so well as in days gone by. He had been dreaming in a confused way – something about rain and elder bloom – when he woke to realise that there was a rabbit lying quietly beside him – no doubt some young buck who had come to ask his advice. The sentry in the run outside should not really have let him in without asking first. Never mind, thought Hazel. He raised his head and said, 'Do you want to talk to me?'

'Yes, that's what I've come for,' replied the other. 'You know me, don't you?'

'Yes, of course,' said Hazel, hoping he would be able to remember his name in a moment. Then he saw that in the darkness of the burrow, the stranger's ears were shining with a faint, silver light. 'Yes, my Lord,' he said. 'Yes, I know you.'

'You've been feeling tired,' said the stranger, 'but I can do something about that. I've come to ask whether you'd care to join my Owsla. We shall be glad to have you and you'll enjoy it. If you're ready, we might go along now.'

They went out past the young sentry, who paid the visitor no attention. The sun was shining and in spite of the cold there were a few bucks and does at silflay, keeping out of the wind as they nibbled the shoots of spring grass. It seemed to Hazel that he would not be needing his body any more, so he left it lying on the edge of the ditch, but stopped for a moment to watch his rabbits and to try to get used to the extraordinary feeling that strength and speed were flowing inexhaustibly out of him into their sleek young bodies and healthy senses.

'You needn't worry about them,' said his companion. 'They'll be all right – and thousands like them. If you'll come along, I'll show you what I mean.'

He reached the top of the bank in a single, powerful leap. Hazel followed; and together they slipped away, running easily down through the wood, where the first primroses were beginning to bloom.

5   Mr Grey's death

Many years and funerals since Daisy Knight Bruce's, I remember brave Mrs Grey. They had not long retired when Mr Grey died.
  'So, Mr Grey has passed away.'

'Isn't it sad about Mr Grey.'
'Poor Mrs Grey . . .'
'Just after he was getting a little better.'
Oh, how they went on.
But Mrs Grey said:
'I'm glad for him, dear, you see he would never have gone on with his garden. He was a good man. I know he is better off where he is.'
That's what Mrs Grey said.
But the others went on.
'It's dreadful about Mr Grey, isn't it?'
They were STILL saying it after the funeral, after singing the hymns and hearing the statement:
Jesus said: THOUGH HE DIE, YET SHALL HE LIVE,
AND WHOEVER LIVES AND BELIEVES IN ME
SHALL NEVER DIE.
So when someone said to me: 'Oh, I do think it is so awfully sad about Mr Grey,' I could bear it no longer. I said: 'But you go to church every Sunday, don't you believe? Whatever do you think church is all about?' And got the reply:
'Well, no one has ever come back, have they?'
'NO ONE HAS EVER COME BACK? JESUS CAME BACK!'
To which I got the answer:
'He was God.'
'But he was MAN!'
At that point it seemed better to mention the jumble sale, and let the Holy Spirit take over.

Anne Shells

SESSION III:11 – I BELONG

From *Rule for a new brother*

> Brother,
> you want to seek God with all your life,
> and love Him with all your heart.
>
> But you would be wrong
> if you thought you could reach Him.
> Your arms are too short, your eyes are too dim,
> your heart and understanding too small.

APPENDIX

To seek God
means first of all
to let yourself be found by Him.
He is the God of Abraham, Isaac and Jacob.
He is the God of Jesus Christ.
He is your God,
not because He is yours
but because you are His.

To choose God
is to realise that you are known and loved
in a way surpassing anything men can imagine,
loved before anyone had thought of you
or spoken your name.

To choose God
means giving yourself up to Him in faith.
Let your life be built on this faith
as on an invisible foundation.
Let yourself be carried by this faith
like a child in its mother's womb.

And so,
don't talk too much about God
but live
in the certainty that He has written your name
on the palm of His hand.
Live your human task
in the liberating certainty
that nothing in the world can separate you
from God's love for you.

Acknowledgements

The publishers are grateful for permission to reproduce the following copyright material.

The Central Board of Finance of the Church of England for the prayers from *Alternative Service Book 1980*.

Clive Sansom, 'The Font', from *Burning Thorn* ed. Griselda Greaves, Hamish Hamilton.

John Hencher, 'Water', *A Place to Dream*, St Paul's.

'Be gentle when you touch bread' and 'Be loving when you drink wine', *Dawn Through Our Darkness*, ed. Giles Harcourt, Wm Collins Sons & Co.

Dear Adults, ed. Christopher Herbert, Church House Publishing for the letters on page 120.

Risen Indeed, ed. Michael Bordeaux, Darton Longman & Todd, for the letter on page 121.

Richard Adams, *Watership Down*, Penguin. Used by permission of David Higham Associates.

'Death, Our Neighbour' by Anne Shells from *This Most Amazing Day*, ed. Christopher Herbert, Church House Publishing, for the passage on Mr Knight's funeral.

Rule for a New Brother, Anon, Darton Longman & Todd; published and copyright 1986.

GOD SPEAKS TO YOU
1. The Old Testament
2. The New Testament

Two fully illustrated, simply written presentations of Bible history, theology and spirituality. The two volumes, sold separately, offer a new concept in Bible study for adolescents and young adults: useful in classrooms, study groups or by individuals.

The text, edited by a noted group of French catechists and biblical experts, presents on each double-page spread:
- A key bible passage, using the Good News Bible
- A note on the context of the passage: when it was written; the literary 'genre'
- An explanation of the passage; why it was written; what it means for Christians then and now
- A simple prayer or 'life application'
- An occasional glossary note

Both volumes
320 × 241mm, 4 colour illustrations, laminated board covers
1. The Old Testament 74pp
0 00 599804 2
2. The New Testament 88pp
0 00 599893 X

ACT JUSTLY
or 15 Drama Sketches to Solve the World's Problems

Compiled by
Martin Leach and Kevin Yell

Fun, action and food for thought: for drama groups with an interest in Third World issues, and for development and Christian groups who would like to try drama.

15 drama sketches, of between 30 seconds and 20 minutes in length, explore topics such as food, debt, water, slavery, social justice and the allocation of resources. Co-published with Christian Aid and CAFOD.

Each drama script is supported by:
- A brief paragraph outlining its subject: land ownership, faith and politics, workers' rights, etc.
- A page of Bible notes: giving scriptural foundation for what is portrayed
- A page of questions and ideas: a thought-provoking action follow-up

200 × 130mm, 128pp, paperback,
0 00 599958 8

BE THOU MY VISION
A Diary of Prayer

Compiled by
Christopher Herbert

Prayer, like talking to friends, can be easy and fun. This book provides thirty-one 'diary days' of prayer. Each day follows the same simple structure of Adoration, Confession, Thanksgiving, Intercession and Dedication. Written especially for older teenagers and young adults, it makes an attractively packaged gift book.

Provides:
- A quote to ponder and meditate, each day
- Free space for users to write down their own thoughts and prayers
- Brief chapters showing how easy prayer can be
- Suggestions on ways of praying and using the scriptures
- 'Arrow Prayers' – short, direct prayers – and other useful prayers

181 × 108mm, 80pp, paperback
Book
0 00 599888 3
Pack of 20
0 00 599931 6